English Literature

Thomas Edward Lawrence

The Scarlet Pimpernel of the Desert

Sommario

Thomas Edward Lawrence,

The scarlet pimpernel of the desert.

PREFACE

This little presentation of Lawrence of Arabia is the fruit both of a work and study path more complex than which could seem. The intention to write a dissertation on such a complex figure of history, considered as a legend by many people, finds his roots on the magic and the romance behind a figure I was fond of since I was young: Thomas Edward Lawrence. A person, which for some aspects, I could feel close for the same way of living, the same attitude towards the challenges and obstacles. Crossing across the reading of the sources, sometimes I was matching myself in the adventures told.

A character of the history, which one hundred years ago almost described the Arab population better than others, finding the features that nowadays are the bases of the fragmentation and crisis in the international landscape. He was talented: he was good at numbers and at people, and this talent, merged with a spark of luck, led T. E. Lawrence to be a legend, a king of the desert. A desert, which helps men discover their own limits. It comes to a desert, where a lot of blood was shred in the past and still today.

There is a passage of C. Keith Chesterton's books, known as the "Four Faultless Felons" written in 1930, which express this concept through the prose.

> *"England has a glorious Empire," said the patriot stoutly "England had a glorious Empire," he said. "So*

had Egypt". The afternoon had already reddened into evening, and the sunset lay in long bands of burning crimson across the purple desolation of that dry inland sea "A glorious Empire", he said "an Empire on which the sun never sets. Look… the sun is setting in blood"[1]

Indeed, studying the history of the Arab revolt, which broke out during the First World War, let be possible to understand many today's scenarios in the international affairs.

However, the cultural and historical interest in this figure, wrapped in a blurred mist of mystery, was not the only reason for choosing this topic, but the desire was to reach the possibility to write something unique about the king of the desert.

The main goal was to reach Lawrence's words becoming true, and not vanity. Concluding the preface, I can start the dissertation on T. E. Lawrence, for the majority known as Lawrence of Arabia, quoting other few sentences, which made him popular.

---

[1] C. Keith Chesterton's Four Faultless felons, https://www.dreame.com/story/1289822464-four-faultless-felons/2187806976, the-man-with-the-green-umbrella.html

"All men dream: but not equally. Those who dream by night

in the dusty recesses of their minds

wake in the day to find that it was vanity: but

the dreamers of the day are dangerous men,

for they may act their dream with open eyes,

to make it possible."

Thomas Edward Lawrence

INTRODUCTION

"All men dream: but not equally. Those who dream by night in the dusty recesses of their minds wake in the day to find that it was vanity: but the dreamers of the day are dangerous men, for they may act their dream with open eyes, to make it possible."[2] *"This I did. I meant to make a new nation, to restore a lost influence, to give Semites the foundations on which to build an inspired dream-place of their national thoughts."*[3]

In the work *"Lawrence by his friends"*, it is possible to find a letter written in September 1916, by Lawrence to Hilda Chaundy, where he wrote that he was ill and he should rest, laying down in his tent in the desert for the all week without doing anything at all, but dreaming.[4] These thoughts and sentences were the content of the letter. Therefore, he started dreaming and dreaming until he felt better. He spent his days in a tent thinking of recovering and in the end standing up. Therefore, he made it. He dreamt to go up until the high Mesopotamian part and he did it. Since that moment, he used

---

[2] T.E. Lawrence, *The Seven Pillars of Wisdom, a Triumph,* Penguins, 1962, p.23. The citation is a fragment of an introduction censored written in the Seven Pillars of Wisdom, starting from the letter sent to his friend Hinda Chaundy.

[3] R. Stephan, *T.E. Lawrence, par Roger Stephan,* collection La Bibliotheque Ideale, Gallimard, 25/04/1960, p.24.

[4] A.W. Lawrence, *T. E. Lawrence by His Friends,* Biography, War Collection, 01.01.1937, p.333. This is the most important collection of memories about T.E. Lawrence and his entire life and works. Edited by his brother Arnold Walter Lawrence.

the first fragment, which later the Oxford printer censored, such a base for his masterpiece's introduction: "The Seven Pillars of Wisdom".[5]

The trimmed down chapters want to depict the mysterious figure of T. E. Lawrence and his path from a dream to a legend, highlighting his pieces of literary works as well. Indeed, beside the role of archaeologist, spy, lieutenant, he was a poet and a writer as well.

In my opinion, it is worth considering this figure in the pool of poets and writers of English literature. He had a simple style of telling the stories. However, what makes him a legend was himself and his capacity to make the desert alive in the English Culture. He took back from the Middle East, not only historical facts, but the essence of the Arab world. Only few people managed to do that. He wrote something that might be contemporary.

The book is composed of three parts. The first one talks about the history of his childhood and the period before becoming a legend. This part defined the various aspects that led to the entrance in action of Lawrence. The second part talks about the Arab revolt and the role of Lawrence in it. It talks about the period spent in the Holy Land and the rise of the legend.

---

[5] R. Stephan, *op.cit*, p.24.

The last part is regarding the last period Lawrence's life and his literature works. This last part makes an overview explaining works and their features. After becoming a legend, Lawrence is also remembered for publishing three important works. The most significant was his account of the Arab revolt in Seven Pillars of Wisdom. Afterwards he wrote the Revolt in the Desert, published in 1927, was an abridged version of Seven Pillars of Wisdom. Then he wrote the unpublished "Mint", divided into three parts and was an account of Lawrence's service in the Royal Air Force. He also devoted himself, once came back from war to the translation of Homer's "Odyssey" and "The Forest Giant".

Eventually, the work ends with an overall opinion and with the closure of the circle started so much time ago. In the end, I wrote the story about one of the historical legends that I admired and that five years ago could seem just a dream, but now it is not vanity; just was meant to be.

T.E. LAWRENCE – A STUDENT, AN ARCHEOLOGIST, A SPY, A KING

The first problem when it comes to the action of depicting the life story of T. E. Lawrence is the absence of bibliography. The story of the character comes from different parts and sources which seems to be enough to recreate that, but actually are not so many as it could seem.

Information is consisting of letters, stories told by his friends, documents and objects recorded at the offices where he worked and principal at all: his books, the most important is The Seven Pillars of Wisdom. Hence, Lawrence's story is the great and central enigma of Lawrence itself.

People that they can truly affirms to be biographers of Lawrence are few and they are i.e. the group at the Intelligence cell at Cairo, the brothers, the addressee of his letters like Charlotte Shaw, Graves, and Thomas.[6]

Even Aldington highlighted that the first and the only witness of Lawrence's speeches and actions is Lawrence himself.[7]

In the life of Lawrence, there was only a woman, beside his mother. It would be strange not to ask why he joined again the Army after his service providing the name of Thomas Shaw.

---

[6] R. Aldington, *Lawrence of Arabia*, Penguin Books, 1971, p.54.
[7] *Ibidem,* p.193.

He met Charlotte Shaw, the wife of Colonel Shaw, for the first time in the apartment in Adelphi terrace, in London. Sir Sydney Cockrell, who was the conservator of the Fitzwilliam Museum in Cambridge, introduced Lawrence at the meeting. They started writing many letters in which Lawrence found his mother figure. They were writing without secrets and brakes as well. Indeed, each of them was expressing their own pure feelings. Charlotte was the only woman to whom Lawrence confided his traumas and secrets. Eventually, Lawrence ended using the surname Shaw to enter the army.[8]

---

[8] Phillip Knightley and Colin Simpson of Robert Laffont, *Les Vie Secretes De Lawrence D'arabia*, 1970. p.367.

Thomas Edward Lawrence was born on 15th of August of 1888[9] in Tremadoc, Caernavonshire. Interestingly, the family registered the dates of his birth the day after, on 16th of August of 1888. He was registered under the Country of Wales and this allowed him to go to a private religious school in Oxford.[10] After his birth, Ned and his family moved to Scotland and then to Dinard in Brittany.[11]

T. E. Lawrence had the fortune to live in a flourishing period for the English Empire. The historical context between 1888 and 1914 seems particularly relevant:

- Britain was a Christian Country, schools taught Christian ethics and judged under Christian standards.

- Britain was a great Imperial Power. British leaders expressed their sense of moral responsibility to provide colonial peoples with competent and fair government. They were using the Christian ethics to fulfil their colonial interests.

- People felt proud to be English, the phenomena called Jingoism, predicated on the superiority of the Englishmen, able to do everything.

---

[9] R. Stephan, *op.cit*, p.16 and R. Aldington, *op.cit.*, p.40.
[10] J. Wilson and National Portrait Gallery, Thomas Edward of Lawrence, Lawrence of Arabia, 1989, p.1. Ned, so-called by his family.
[11] R. Aldington, *op.cit.*, p.41.

- British colonial rulers practised 'indirect rule'. They tried to work through existing structures, maintaining the status of local chiefs.

- Overt British patriotism was at its zenith. Upper and middle-class young men were educated to help rule and defend Britain's immense and diverse empire. They learned the virtue of leading by personal example. Lawrence was one of the many young men to volunteer for the Officers Training Corps, when was founded in 1912.

- The obligation of personal excellence extended beyond values and attitudes to physical fitness activities. The Boy Scouts movement was in 1907 a new important entity.

- Sexual abstinence was the only effective form of contraception, sexual activity of any kind, outside the marriage, was immoral and almost certainly a threat to health.

- Life-long social rejection of anyone known to be illegitimate was a corollary of the previous point, which is one of the Lawrence's traumas in life.

- Victorian England was adventurous and inventive. The industrial revolution had launched the ever-accelerating advance of technology. During Lawrence's youth, engineering was still an exciting novelty. He lived in a world only recently transformed by railways and steam ships. Motor cars and aeroplanes were symbols in their infancy.

- Today, people think of the Middle East both as a war-torn and as rich of oil. Neither was true before the First World War. In England, the Middle East was revered as the Holy Land and was known mainly thanks to travellers' accounts and exotic images such as the lithographs by David Roberts published in the mid-19th century.

- Oil was first commercially in Iran in 1911, and before the First World War, was known to be present in parts of Iraq (then Mesopotamia). It was not discovered in commercial quantities in Bahrain until 1932 and in Saudi Arabia until 1938. During the period that Lawrence was involved, the prospect of oil discovery played no part in British policy towards areas of the Middle East outside Iran and Mesopotamia.[12]

---

[12] J. Wilson, *T. E. Lawrence: from dream to legend*, 2009, 2011, http://www.telstudies.org/discussion/youth_1888-1914/wilson_tel_from_dream_to_legend.shtml , visited on 2019, p.2. This paper was written for a T. E. Lawrence conference held in Oldenburg, Germany, in October 2009. It has been published in German translation, as 'T. E. Lawrence: Vom Traum zur Legende', in the catalogue to the exhibition Lawrence von Arabien Genese eines Mythos (Mainz, Philipp von Zabern, 2010 pp. 17-26). The Castle Hill Press subscribers' newsletter on 2 December 2011 posted this revised English version.

He was lucky to gain knowledge, which no one had at that moment, his travels were something extraordinary, they were the centre of interest of the great Powers.

Otherwise, it was not only fortune, he had also a strong will power, he was good at number and at languages and he had an excellent memory. He was strong and active. He liked cycling, swimming, canoeing and wrestling with other boys.[13]

He had a big head, probably bigger than normal; his body was smaller because of an accident when he was young. Indeed, he fought with a boy and he broke his leg. This shock did not allow the body to develop normally. He had blond hair and blue, almost penetrating, crystal eyes.[14]

He was intellectually gifted showing high scores across a wide range of subjects, and exceptional ability in English and religious studies. Lawrence had an original, observant and creative mind with a quick grasp of practical questions. He could absorb large amounts of information and draw interesting conclusions.

He was not impressive - at least at first glance. He was only 1m 66 tall. Short stature was a disadvantage in competitive school sports, but he was proud of his strength and fitness and the distances and speeds he achieved on his bicycle.

---

[13] R. Aldington, *op.cit*, p.51.
[14] *Ibidem*, p.54.

These often-solitary exploits reflected one of the most remarkable facets of his personality. He had inherited from his mother an iron will power. It extended his physical endurance far beyond the point where most people would give up.

By all accounts, his eyes were remarkable. Many people found them commanding. When he cared to use it, he had astonishing persuasive power.

He learned photography from his father. He studied the design and construction of mediaeval castles and used photographs to record interesting details and his mind was naturally inquisitive. Throughout his life, his writing shows the observation skills acquired during his youth, and his wish to understand the underlying structure and mechanism of what he saw.

His letters contain ample evidence of ambition, though in the pre-war years he seemed to lack any goal except writing and travelling.

Small stature may also have prompted an irritating trait he recognised in himself: a tendency to seek attention through eccentric behaviour, particularly when dealing with strangers.[15]

He had a strong and extroverted personality and he had a great charm and energy. He merged his talent with his fortune,

---

[15] J. Wilson, op.cit., description of the paper from a dream to a legend, p.3.

smoothing his imperfections and creating a legend following what Leonardo da Vinci said: *"the wisdom is the daughter of the experience"*.[16] Indeed, in order to be a legend people should combine knowledge and wisdom to make an impact.[17] This is what Lawrence did: he combined the knowledge he got with the experience to make him remembered.

It could be interesting asking how it was possible to achieve such a great passion for such a little man. Churchill defined him as one of the best men of our times.[18] His notes are spread all around the World; the bibliography is made of letters, which were written by him and his friends, or consisting of documents stored nearby the Public Record Office of London, and more other offices.

It was possible to find sources in Turkey, or in Israel, where a meeting between Feisal, who was designed as king of Arabs, and Chaim Weizmann, the Zionist founder of Israel, took place concerning the future of the Arabic peninsula.

Anyway, for someone he was not a legend, but just taking advantages of the passing of events. An example could be the book of Richard Aldington, in which he tried to break down the legend of Lawrence of Arabia and to show that he was just an impostor.

---

[16] Leonardo da Vinci's sentence.
[17] Pep talk at the USNA, American Naval Academy.
[18] P. Knightley and C. Simpson, *op.cit.*, p.10.

Not only Aldington did not consider Lawrence as a hero, because he just turned all his events to his part, but even as a writer. Indeed, in Aldington perception Lawrence's work might be considered as a work of the imagination rather than history.[19] He reported some notes from diaries written during 1915-1916 where Lawrence affirmed that even since his childhood; he had wanted to be a hero and that was always matter of fighting between rushing into limelight and hiding in utter darkness, but considering the limelight as always that part winning.

However, Aldington studied the subject on the bases of his prejudice, so the revulsion against Lawrence was intensified.[20]

Moreover, Aldington believed that the reason for Lawrence misuse of talent and behaviour was based on his disturb conditions provoked by two incidents in his life: the first one the discovery of illegitimacy born and the second in 1917, during his adventure in Deera. Although in my opinion, there were more causes at the base of the Lawrence's behaviour.[21]

Before to start writing about the history of the enfant considered as "estrange" for his age, it is quite important to write about his family, which was an important knot in the

---

[19] R. Aldington, *op.cit.*, p.19.
[20] *Ibidem*, p.28.
[21] *Ibidem*, p.16.

growth of the child, as well as other traumas that signed Lawrence's life.

Sir Ronald Storrs wrote an article on the life and the born of T. E. Lawrence.[22] He wrote that he was the second son out of five sons, after the first marriage of the father, who had already four daughters.[23]

He was the son of Thomas Robert Tighe Chapman, who was born on 6th of November of 1846. He married in 1873 for the first time, and he had between 1874 and 1881 four daughters with his legal wife and then the boys with his scots girl, presumably Sarah Maden, that as it results from the part written by Sir Ronald Storrs resulted written in the Lawrence's birth certificate. Sarah Maden was the daughter of a Sunderland engineer, his mother gives her date of birth in 1861, but no Maden appeared in national records. There was a Sarah Maden recorded in 1863 in the Country of Lancaster, but she was a different person. Indeed, in the brother's certificates the name of Sarah Juner appeared. She was born on 31st of August of 1861 in Sunderland. Lawrence's father, indeed, had another woman, which gave him the other 5 sons.

Thomas Robert Tighe Chapman later took the name of Thomas Robert Lawrence and moved to another Country; in order to go and live with the other woman in 1884, Since Mrs Chapman

---

[22] R. Aldington, *op.cit.*, p.35.
[23] R. Stephan, *op.cit.*, p.16, and R. Aldington, *ibidem*, p.40.

refused to grant her husband the divorce. The second woman was Sarah Juner.[24]

T. R. T. Chapman was the second of four sons, the family was living at Hills and Sanders and, after the death of his elder brother, he continued to live there with his first wife: Edith Rochfart Boyd. They had four daughters; Eva, rose, Florence, Mabel. After the marriage Mrs Chapman became bitter and fanatical religious, consequently Mr Chapman started drinking heavily and having affairs with the new woman.[25]

T. R. Lawrence was a skilled amateur photographer, using a professional-standard camera (now in Oxford's Museum of the History of Science), who liked sailing and shooting. Lawrence's mother was strong-willed and practical. Lawrence once described her as a fanatical homemaker. Both parents were deeply religious and the Sundays, the all family attended St. Aldgate's church in Oxford and said prayers daily at home.[26]

Notwithstanding the situation of Lawrence's birth was a secret, it remained a problem for the interaction with the society.

Fortunately, the consequences had simply effects on the personality and an inner level of Lawrence personality. In a

---

[24] *Ibidem,* p.15.
[25] J. Wilson and National Portrait Gallery, *op.cit.,* p.6.
[26] J. Wilson, *op.cit.,* p.2.

letter addressed to Charlotte Shaw[27], that nowadays are available to the public at the library of the British Museum, he wrote, when he was exiled in Karachi on 14th of April of 1927, that *"He always maintained the secret, by saying half of the truth. He was supposed to say it when he would have achieved a huge notoriety".*[28]

Lawrence had four brothers Frank, Arnold, Bob and Will. The picture comes from the collection of the Professor A. W. Lawrence.[29]

---

[27] In Mrs Shaw Lawrence seemed to find the only possible relationship with a woman, considering her as his mother.

[28] R. Aldington, *op.cit.*, p.40.

[29] P. Knightley and C. Simpson, op.cit., p.25.

HIS TRAUMAS

The first trauma I underlined, in accordance with the social life and the customs of the Victorian period, was the illegitimacy, which led Lawrence not to marry; he told his parents that he would not have children.

Wilson reported that in that period the illegitimacy was a significant stigma in the respectable environment, profession, and social status. In order to avoid the problem, Lawrence always said that his parents should have had no children and that spent in occupations where damage were potentially minimal.[30]

The second one was the leg broken after a fight at school. Indeed, Aldington in his book reports that the arrest in Lawrence's physical development was officially attributed to the shock of his leg broken at school.[31]

Suleiman Mousa reports also this episode of Lawrence's life from which is possible to connect with his strong will and determination.

"When he was 16 years old, he engaged a scuffle with an older student, and he emerged with a broken leg. This accident retarded the growth and from that moment he remained short".[32]

---

[30] J. Wilson, *op.cit., p.4.*
[31] R. Aldington, *op.cit.,* p.395.
[32] Suleiman Mousa, *T.E. Lawrence an Arab view*, translated by Albert Butros, London, Oxford University press 1966. p.3.

He always wanted to test his limits, in fact he tried to test his endurance, trying not to eat, but without stopping to work and train for few days. In the lapse between School and University, he served as a voluntary the royal artillery for 6 months, but his family did not know about that.

In addition to these traumas, I would add the trauma with Janet Laurie, a girl with who Lawrence fell in love. Unfortunately, she told that, one night, without warning or courtship, she turned laughing down the proposal of Lawrence. [33]

Eventually, another trauma in his life was the situation of arresting and capturing nearby *Deera* on 20th of November of 1917 in front of the ruins of *Fort Azrka*. He told the episode to Rolls and then he wrote about that in his book from the moment Turks captured him with the excuse of recruiting and disserting the Turk Army until the moment with the guards passing through a violent interview that probably ended in a rape perpetrated by the Turk security forces. Indeed, he wrote each moment of the event until he lost consciousness. He woke up later with the wounds and the pain in a black cell. He wrote to Charlotte Shaw on 26th of March of 1924 that he lost his body integrity, the citadel of his integrity had been lost.[34]

---

[33] J. Wilson and National Portrait Gallery, *op.cit.*, p.4.
[34] T.E. Lawrence, op.cit., the Seven Pillars of Wisdom, p.454-456.

Notwithstanding all the traumas he passed through, he used his strong willpower to go further and get to point. Since he was young, he had always shown an interest in culture, literature and archaeology.

He won prizes and scholarships who let him study and what he learnt out of school and University was more important to his life than what he learnt on books. When he was around 15 years old, he had already gained from his father the interest in archaeology. Gradually Lawrence concentrated on the Gothic Architecture and especially medieval castles and fortifications.[35]

When he was about 16, he also studied the Art of War, with the possibility to study Clausewitz, Mahan, Foch and other military thinkers of the Age, even if he had his own style to fight.

Therefore, in 1905, he left England to travel alone and the adventure was like a dream for him. He started visiting the castles in France because he was fond of medieval castles for passion and scholar interest.[36]

---

[35] *Ibidem, p.47.*
[36] R. Stephan, *op.cit.,* p.17.

Then thanks to the people he met and the right scholarships he won, he was spurred to study also those castles in Syria and Palestine.

Lawrence chose *"the influence of the Crusades on Medieval European military architecture"* like subject for his graduation thesis, because he had already gathered a lot of information[37], but also probably because at the University history of the Crusades was his special and favourite subject.[38]

From there, in 1909 Lawrence spent the summer in Syria and Palestine, visiting crusader castles for his Oxford thesis. He took off in June 1909 and flew to Beirut, where he started learning a little bit of Arabic. In September 1909, he went to *Nazareth, Harosheth, Athlit, Haifa, Acre, Kaarn, Tyr, Sidon,* as well as, he passed by *Lattaquie* and Aleppo. After he had walked 1700 kilometres on foot for three months gathering information, drawings and pictures, he decided to come back England, especially after the attack of Kurds, where for the first time he was really in danger.

When he was in Syria, he wanted to visit on foot all the places and castles of the area. For his protection, Lawrence was carrying a letter called *irade*, which was released by the Turkish Government ordering all local officers to give him help or aids and it was obtained by the head of his college Sir

---

[37] S. Mousa, *op.cit., p.4.*
[38] R. Aldington, *op.cit., p.68.*

John Rhys, with the help of Lord Curzon, who at the time worked at the Consulate of Turkey.[39]

After his travel in Syria to look with his own eyes the castles of crusades, in 1910 he came back England and he made 3 travels to France, the first in June, the second in August with his brother Frank and in November to see the collection of medieval pottery in Rouen.[40] At the end of the year, his thesis was presented at Oxford, shortly after his return, and the thesis was praised with a prize that allowed him to get with a little budget the possibility to join later the British museum excavation at Jerablus, which was the fortress city of the Hittite Empire, called Carchemish.[41]

Eventually, his first thesis became a book, known as Crusades Castles, in which is possible to find not only considerations, but also draws and pictures made by Lawrence himself like product of the research.

"The Crusades castles" was one of the first work of Lawrence when he was still a young scholar and for this reason the work could be considered still bitter enough. But the importance lays on the possibility to find all the illusions and the dreams, which were born in the heart of the young Oxfordian student that was living amid adventures, skylines, glory, in the middle of the

---

[39] S. Mousa, *op.cit.*, p.4.
[40] R. Stephan, *op.cit.*, p.18.
[41] S. Mousa, *op.cit.*, p.5.

desert, place where centuries before many crusades and battles had been fought.[42]

The original study of Lawrence on crusades castles was based on the idea he verified that all castles, even those more ancient, posed on the centre of their design the donjon or the *prygos* (tower), this was the type of castle used to be built on the western Countries. Some castles of Crusaders followed these features as well, which identified some examples like the castles of Beaufort and Tripoli.[43]

He also defined how simple would be to modify the castle, starting from a normal and geometrical one. The fortress of *Yibna (Ibelin)* and the *Blanchegarde (Tall al-Safi)* are examples of these constructions.

The Castle of *Darum (Dayr al-Balah)* on the south side of Gaza was another example how castle was developing. In the 1170 King *Amalric I,* king of Jerusalem, built a fortress of modest dimensions, with four towers on each corner and one of them was bigger and more solid than the other ones. In 1170, Saladin's soldiers managed to enter the castle but occupying just the lower floor, while the resident troops backed in the upper one, building later other defences.

---

[42] T. E. Lawrence, *Crusades Castles*, preface by Franco Cardini, Introduction by Denys Pringle, CAHIERS, Castelvecchi, 2018, Translation by Maria Grazia, Chiappori, Roma. p.XVI.
[43] *Ibidem,* p.25.

However, in 1187, after the war of Hattin, Saladin conquered the castle. Four years later in 1191, the parts changed again, Arabs gave up against Riccardo I. The story told that Riccardo I allowed them to reconstruct the changes of the castle, which passed through between years 1170 and 1191. In the end, there were 17 towers and a mot. The idea was simply to add other walls outside the core, concentrically around the principal one. Lawrence noticed that the two castles previously mentioned had similar basis to those coming from Byzantine period.[44]

Lawrence presented his work "the Crusades castles" as the Oxfordian thesis of his degree, and then stored in the Bodleian Library in Oxford, where there are some notes (*res C52, envelop 8*) that for sure they represent the first draft of the thesis. He was suggesting that crusaders brought to Arabia the style of Norman Donjon. At the beginning, the style was simple, but then, when Riccardo I and Luigi IX started visiting Syria, they changed it and improved the infrastructures.[45]

In 1911, he wrote a short dissertation on the strategic position of crusades castles, on which he reported the defensive strategy adopted by crusaders in the cities of East. The aim of this short dissertation was to help a friend, Leonard Green, who should have some conference in Oxford.

---

[44] *Ibidem.* p.28-34.
[45] *Ibidem,* p.187.

He wrote a letter from *Jubayl* to Green on 14th of January of 1911. The letter's content was saying that the most awesome thing of Syria was the wildness of places, which were difficult to reach and full of natural obstacles. It was full of *"wadi"* and hills where passages were extremely narrows due to the presence of huge stones and beds of rivers, which are steep and deep. Horses cannot carry huge amount of goods and neither go to scour, reconnoitre or defend from surprise attacks.[46]

He described the geography and then depicted the city of Urfa, until the day within was under crusaders and resulted complicate to expunge. Moreover, the letter reported some extremely interesting examples with other castles such as *the Crac des chevaliers*[47] (*Kalaat el-Hosn*), *Chastel Blanc* and *Aarka.*[48]

In the end of the letter, he made a little error, indeed, reading the notes and the study of his brother about the castle of *Baghras*, Lawrence told that there were two big castles protecting the place, *Beilan* and *Baghras*, but it was just *Baghras.*[49]

Here is the point where life of Lawrence changed: the meeting at Magdalen College with the future Commander David

---

[46] *Ibidem,* p.201.
[47] In T. E. Lawrence of J. Wilson, Lawrence sent a letter to his mother, 29.08.1909, home letters, p. 105. He wrote that he thought that he found the finest castle in the world.
[48] *Ibidem,* p.201-204.
[49] *Ibidem.*

George Hogarth, who was interested not in Lawrence's experience as much as he could be interested in his aptitude, his knowledge of the places and Arabic.[50] He won a scholarship for studying ancient pottery and there was the chance to go to Carchemish to start his research, which was boosted by David George Hogarth, because he hoped to train Lawrence up as his successor; he was brilliant and curious.[51]

D. G. Hogarth was the Director of Ashmolean Museum. He worked for the Intelligence Service, more precisely for the naval intelligence, he went to the high part of the Mesopotamia, seeking for the crusades vestigial of the first realm created abroad by Frances. I am talking about the Count of Edessa, that Baldwin of Boulogne, brother of Godfrey of Boulogne, and future king of Jerusalem, founded in 1098, conquered from the Armenian princess that owned it in that moment. Indeed, it was Edessa, nowadays called Urfa, the metropolis and the holy place of the Armenian ethnic population: remembered as the city of Abraham and Nimrud as well.[52]

---

[50] This desire is possible to see in the paper of J. Wilson. He wrote in his paper that: "The career - perhaps pastime would be a better word - that Lawrence first chose was archaeology. His mentor was D. G. Hogarth, Keeper of Oxford's Ashmolean Museum. In 1910, shortly before Hogarth and Lawrence met, Macmillan published Hogarth's memoir Accidents of an Antiquary's Life. In it, he wrote: 'Your true Antiquary is born, not made.'

[51] R. Aldington, *op.cit.,* p.100.

[52] F. Cardini, op.cit., p.VI – VIII.

Hogarth was overseeing the expedition until the year 1912, year when Leonard Woolley replaced him.[53]

---

[53] J. Wilson and National Portrait gallery, op.cit., p.31.

ARRIVAL AT THE HOLY LAND – THE RISE OF A LEGEND

Before telling the history of Lawrence when he arrived for the second time in Arabia, it is necessary to depict, as well as I did for the history moment in which Lawrence lived, the situation in Arabia, the society and the geography. In fact, from here it is possible to look at the problems and features that exist nowadays. In my opinion, since the XX Century had begun with the Sykes-Picot agreements, the meetings between Arabs and Zionist, the colonial ideas of Englishmen, Russians, French and Jews, the complexity and paradoxically the simplicity of the tribes that were living in the desert clashed into inner negative consequences. People who were leading had no idea of what could come forward.

The situation in Arabia was different from how nowadays is, indeed, it was not full of people travelling to enjoy luxury or to invest money in enormous firms, agencies, or oil industry.

There were more subtle games and interests, first at all; there was the construction of a railway leading from Berlin to Bagdad, then, the interests on the Red Sea and Indian Ocean.

In Arabia, there were at least 10 chieftains[54]:

-        *MUNTAFIK,* ruled by *IBN SADU*, pro Turks and Germans;

---

[54] R. Aldington, *op.cit.,* p.173.

- *KUWAIT,* ruled by *IBN SABA,* paid by the British Council;

- *BHAREIN,* ruled by *IBN KALIFA,* paid by India;

- *OMAN,* ruled by *IBN SAID,* paid by India;

- *HADRAMAUT,* ruled by *IBN AUDA*;

- *YEMEN,* ruled by holy man, the *IMAM IBN MOHAMED HAMID*;

- *ASIR,* ruled by *IBN ALI EL IDRASSI,* the British Council in Egypt;

- *SHAMMAR,* ruled by *IBN RASHID*;

- *NEJD,* ruled in RIADR, ruled by *IBN SAUD.*

- HEJAZ and the area of the Holy cities such as MEDINA, MECCA,

- YENBO, AL WEJH, and JEDDA were ruled by the Emir *HUSSEIN IBN ALI* descending of the Hashemites. SHARIF had four sons: Ali, Abdullah, Feisal and Said.[55]

The sense of freedom and desire for an independence from the maleficent Turks, which were stressing the life of these tribes in the first period of XX century, was the spark to catch the mass and boost populations to rise and get their own independence. Hussein gave his availability to the British Empire for a mutual collaboration. However, England agreed

---

[55] *Ibidem,* p.173-173.

only in 1915, when the Crisis of Gallipoli broke out and they found a way to exploit this situation even with the secret agreement of Sykes-Picot, wherein the truly intentions of the Powers were defined.

The truly intents were: 1) to replace the predominance of the Turkish Empire with the English one; 2) to divide the tribes and consequently the Imperial heredity would have been shared in many parts, following the roman dictum *"dividi et impera"*. It was only in this way that the Empire could exploit efficiently the oil areas.[56]

Charles M. Doughty should be recalled for his travels in the wild and terrifying desert. Doughty's book starts with an introduction of T. E. Lawrence, who in the introduction highlighted that he studied Arabia Desert for ten years and that the book was not like others, it was brilliant for what was written by Doughty. This book might be considered as the first and indispensable work upon the Arabs of the desert; the more you travel there, the greater the respect for the insight and the judgments on the book.[57]

For this reason, Lawrence believed that the places in Arabia are to live. In addition, in accordance with Lawrence, Doughty wrote with words and phrases fitted to those places, which cannot be dissociated that Arabia even if was the land with its

---

[56] F. Cardini, *op.cit.,* p. IX.
[57] C. M. Doughty, *Travels in Arabia Desert*, with an introduction by T. E. Lawrence, Volume I, Dover Publication, Canada, 1979, p.17.

smells and dirty; it was also the land with its nobility and its freedom.[58]

With the arrival of the Turks, Arab happiness became a dream. Semites of Asia passed under the Turkish yoke and found that it was a slow death. Turkish stripped their goods, their spirit shrived in the numbing breath of a military Government. Turkish politics were crude and there was no sense for patriotism, the Arab language was banished.[59]

Doughty tried to tell the full and exact truth of all he saw. Doughty was impressed by the strange virtues, which he identified in isolation and independence of those people.

There was an expression regarding their faults: *"if one lives any time with the Arabs, he will have in his life after a feeling of the desert"*. Doughty, as well as Lawrence, experienced the feeling of nomadism, making the strongest and most determinate man. Lawrence wrote in a letter to his mother that he became Arab in habits, adding that he was walking alone in the middle of the desert, living as an Arab among Arabs.[60]

In the second chapter of his masterpiece, which is The Seven Pillars of Wisdom, Lawrence started the description of what Arab may be. Should be considered a population under a same

---

[58]*Ibidem,* p. 17-21.
[59] T. E. Lawrence, op.cit., p.42.
[60] S. Mousa, *op.cit.,* p.4.

language, but to understand their revolt and their present social behaviours is important grasping by looking at their geography. Indeed, the natural environment in which the dwellers lived, changing from a valley to another had radical consequences in the structure of the tribes and their growth.[61]

The desert is characterizing the Arabic Peninsula, between the west oases and the hills there is the Nejd Desert, an area of gravel and lava, in the south part there is some sand that makes difficult the way and in the north side there is a belt of sand before an immense plain valley of gravel and lava.[62]

The population is made of Bedouins which wandering from a place to another and making their economy with the supply produced by camels and what they can have moving from a place to another.[63]

Doughty supposed that people who lived in the desert saw the world always in line, with two colours, white or black; they knew only the truth and the untruth, belief and unbelief.[64]

For Lawrence people in the desert were narrow-minded people, whose imaginations were keen but not creative. Their convictions were by instinct and their activities were led by intuitions. Their profound reaction against matter led them to preach barrenness, renunciation and poverty. In the desert, the

---

[61] T. E. Lawrence, op.cit., p.31, Chapter II.
[62] *Ibidem*, p.32.
[63] *Ibidem*, p.34.
[64] C. M. Doughty, *op.cit,* p.21.

Bedouin finds himself free, losing natural ties or comforting superfluities and complications. Coffee, water and women were the only vices the Bedouin enjoyed. In his life, there is air, sun, wind, sometimes silence but all the time huge spaces with their emptiness, and this is the key. The Bedouin lives his own life in a hard selfishness. He finds luxury in abnegation, renunciation and self-restraint.[65]

Doughty went among these people and assimilated the way of being in the way he could considered himself as an Arab in manners and a European in mind, maintaining in this way a perfect judgement. When he came back, he took with him his notebook, where he wrote word for words the life of Arabs, the soul of the desert, the complete existence of a remarkable and self-contained community, shut away from the rest of the world.[66]

He was writing about a social organization that was developing in the area of the desert and where the only efficient manner life's organization was in tribes, partly because of original family feelings, partly because self-preservation instinct. Each tribe had its district in the desert. The extent and the nature of these tribal districts were determinate by the economic laws of camel breeding.[67]

---

[65] *Ibidem*, p.22.
[66] *Ibidem*, p.23.
[67] *Ibidem*, p.24.

However, the international situation was changing and, in few years, would have showed his effects and broke the balance of the regions. In particular, the penetration of Germany in Middle East was more evident. They wanted to build a super railway until Bagdad and the giant that could help them was the Turkish Empire, which became allied.

After he had graduated, he had won the scholarship at the Magdalene University and Hogarth, accepted him in December 1910. He started his new adventure and went to *Jebail* to improve his Arabic, before joining the British Museum's excavations at Carchemish, village close to Jerablus on the River Euphrates. Carchemish was amid the coast of the river Euphrates and his valleys. He worked at Carchemish until the spring of 1914.[68]

When he was in Syria, he learned some Arabic, especially the vulgar forms, and for this reason, Hogarth wanted to add him to the expedition to Carchemish yet.

To get prepared to the excavation, the Museum decided to send him again in Middle East, in Lebanon, where he took additional classes of Arabic from Miss *Fareedah al-Akle*, and then he moved to Haifa and from there by train to Damascus, passing through Aleppo and arriving at Carchemish.

Unfortunately, in Carchemish, there was another archaeologist more prepared and, in relation to the studies of Lawrence, and the availability for the vacancy, Lawrence oversaw the pottery work, photography and keeping some records of elements founded.[69]

---

[68] J. Wilson, *op.cit., p 5.*
[69] S. Mousa, *op.cit.,* p.5.

During this period, Lawrence had the opportunity to stay in contact with Arabs, to stay among them and learn. His success was in the ability to penetrate the inner self of the Arab individual.

He wrote in his masterpiece *The Seven Pillars of Wisdom*:

> *"Among the Arabs there were no distinctions, traditional or natural, except the unconscious power given a famous sheikh by virtue of his accomplishment; and they taught me that no man could be their leader except he ate the rank's food, wore their cloths, and lived level with them".*[70]

Until the 1913, Thompson was working at Carchemish, when Woolley replaced him. Woolley is one of the few people, who were important in the life of T. E. Lawrence.

The cemeteries of the first Millennium near *Deve Huyuk* were the most important archaeological site in Carchemish.

At that moment, the *Deve Huyutuk* cemeteries rescue regarded the prevention against peasants, who were looting graveyards revealed by cuttings for the Berlin-Baghdad railway. During February, March and April 1913, it was clear that there was a competition among dealers of Aleppo and the expedition under

---

[70] T. E. Lawrence, op.cit., *p.157.*

the name of Madame Koch, which is the first mover for the excavation in the Hittite cemetery.[71]

What they found was many axes, spears, T.E. Lawrence thought it was Bronze, but the truth was that it was iron.

Among the objects in the *Deve Huyuk II* graves, pronounced Iranian characteristics were evident in several cases. Among the pottery, two types were relevant here: some lamps in an extremely coarse red ware, conspicuously different both from the imported Greek fabrics and from the local buff wares were totally unlike anything in the ceramic repertory.

Bowl ring burnished fabric and zoomorphic Jars were typical of the middle Bronze Age in the region of Carchemish.[72]

---

[71] P.R.S. MOOREY, Cementeries of the First Millennium B.C. At Deve Huyuk 1980, Near Carchemish (Jerablus), Salvaged by T. E. Lawerence And C. L. Wolley 1913. The picture is printed in page 15.
[72] *Ibidem,* p.25.

It is important to introduce another important character of the desert, the so-called queen of the desert: Gertrude Bell. She was important in the life of Lawrence for the suggestion she gave about the publication of his works. She came to visit the Carchemish expedition in Hogarth's absence. In Avril 1911, Hogarth came back London and left the work to Lawrence who was updating Hogarth with his letters. The letter n° 30 of 23rd of May of 1911 to his mother reports that he was using a new camera, which allowed him to watch things better than the human eyes 2000 times better.[73]

After Bell had been with Germans at *Ashus*, she said that English had prehistoric methods of research. Lawrence was in charge of pottery, but reports of his superiors were saying that he had spent part of the time playing. This was because he used to finish his work fast and, for this reason, he had more spare time to stay with other Arabs working there.[74]

Woolley said that Lawrence was good with Arab workers: e.g. he invented a competition such a way to maintain the order, to be more effective in the conclusion of the tasks, and achieving the result prefixed. Creating a competition among them, he spurred the divided groups, which aim was to reach to the result faster than other groups for the compensation. The result was impressive, indeed, the time of work passed from twelve

---

[73] P. Knightley and C. Simpson, op.cit., p. 98.
[74] R. Aldington, *op.cit.*, p.102.

hours in one hour. He started understanding the colloquial and dialectic Arab. [75]

At Carchemish, he gained both understanding and respect for the people among whom he lived and worked. From Lawrence's letters can be said that he was strongly influenced in those first years by the idea of the *'noble savage'*. He felt that Europeans had much to learn from the simpler lifestyle of the Arab peasantry - and even more from the life of the Bedouin.

With his behaviour and dress, he became the most popular foreign character known in Arabia. He spent many hours listening to Arab people working. Buchan defined him in 1916, like that person that was able to merge in the population and be accepted by that. He made a conscious effort, in the years before the war, to explore Arab life and culture. He saw how the corrupt Turkish officials exploited them and wished they could be free to govern themselves.

In his opinion there was a big enough educated class in both Syria and Mesopotamia to provide Arab administrations. [76]

In July 1911, after the conclusion of expedition in Carchemish, Lawrence spent 4 months exploring on foot the region in the northeast side of Euphrates. He started his journey from Tall-

---

[75] *Ibidem,* p.6.
[76] J. Wilson, *op.cit.,* p.6. Even in P. Knightley and C. Simpson, op.cit., p.61-62.

Ahmar and visited the castles of *Urfa (Edessa), Harranm Birijik (al-Bira), Rum Kalaat and Tall Bashir*. He jotted down all his notes in a diary written by pencil, which would be later published in 1937 under the name of *"The Diary of T. E. Lawrence"*, by A. W. Lawrence in 1939.[77]

From 14th to 16th of July, he visited the castle of Urfa, he stayed in a khan, and one day an agent of the police waited for him outside the tent, suggesting that he would have needed a *zaptieh* (i.e. watch guard). [78]

The day after he met once again the police officer, who found him a *zaptieh*. He found out that the castle was almost completely Arab, with just the particularity of the mot, which origins are romans.[79]

On 17th of July, he moved towards Harran, where he deeply analysed the castle. Lawrence saw the tower of the Cathedral from far away because it was big. He entered and he found inside the sheik, who did that place his house. He visited the inner part during the day of 17th and the day after, on 18th of July, he visited the outside. He started again his travel and on Saturday 22nd of July, he visited the castle *Birijik Castle, (al Bira)*. Afterwards on 24th of July, at 10 am he arrived at *Rum Kalaat*. On 25th of July, he woke up at 3:45 am to take a bath

---

[77] F. Cardini, *op.cit.*, p.205-206.
[78] *Ibidem*, p.206.
[79] *Ibidem*, p.207-209.

in the river and then to move, he proceed towards *Tall Bashar*, where he stayed for short time.[80]

During this time, Lawrence was considering his period of life fantastic, instead of what he thought during his stay at Cairo, considering that period such a glorious one.[81]

Returning to Jerablus from a walking tour between digging seasons in 1911, Lawrence became extremely ill. Two villagers who worked on the excavations nursed him back to health and he owed them his life. Afterwards, he made the more intelligent of the two, a boy nicknamed Dahoum, his personal assistant. In his life this young worker called Dahoum, Sheik Ahmed the real name, would play an important role in Lawrence's life.[82]

However, his friendship had not been a good thing in his future. Nevertheless, even if it was scandalous, Lawrence did not try to dissipate.[83]

Aldington made too strong judgements and highlighted the fault of Lawrence. Aldington wrote in his inquiry that the "Great Love" of Lawrence's life was the "donkey boy", called Dahoum, known as Sheik Ahmed. The other friend was the Foreman Hamaudi: he was tall, he had a large body and he was immensely powerful. Lawrence and Sheik were like brothers.

---

[80] *Ibidem*, p.210-213.
[81] R. Aldington, op.cit., p.120.
[82] P. Knightley and C. Simpson, op.cit., p.75-80.
[83] R. Stephan, op.cit., p.17.

In fact, Sheik was younger than Lawrence was and the young boy was 15 when they met each other for the first time.[84]

Lawrence brought them with him to Oxford once for 2 weeks in July 1913. Before that, they travelled in the holy land of Middle East: they left Gaza on the 7th of January of 1913 and led to Aqaba following the trimmed down itinerary.[85]

At first, they passed through the villages and tents in the region of *Birseba*, this knowledge during the war is going to be vital for English troops. After that, they went through the mountain *Abda*.[86]

From the stories told by Lawrence, the Desert was a place inhospitable, hostile and the tribes during the invasion under the name of Mahomet decided to change the place. These tribes were *Tiyaha, Alaouin, Terabin, Azazma.* The environment was wild, and the surface of the terrain was made of calcar that offered a resistant shield from the wind and the rain. It was a hard rock, extracted for the creation of necklace, which was possible to find in *Abda* and used for the construction of byzantine houses.

In the North of the region of *Biresba* the calcar is softer and plenty of siliceous, different from the previous calcar, which was rich of diorites. This is useful when it rains that let the

---

[84] R. Aldington, op.cit., p.120-130.
[85] C.L. Woolley et T.E. Lawrence, *Le Desert de Sin,* introduction of Sir Frederic Kenyon, Payot, Paris 1927, p.68.
[86] *Ibidem, p.24 and 25, images VI and VII.*

siliceous enter the terrain and make it fertile. Unfortunately, when the wind arrives sometimes there may be the creation of sandstorms. The only vegetation that survives in the Meridional desert is made of plants that are parasite and normally it is possible to see trees called *ethyl* and *butmeh*, which are useless.[87]

The *Darb-el-Chour* that made famous Abraham and Isaac was the route used to cross the desert. In addition to this route, what makes famous this desert in the north part is the *Tell* that is an artificial Mountain with a castle, such like a fort on the top. The most famous is the *Tell - el - Milah*. Beside the Egypt border there is the *Ain Kadeis*, that is a massive white mountain.[88] The oasis Ain Moueilleh, considered as a departures point, is a vital knot on the logistical map.[89]

In the end of 1913 when Lawrence was back, Woolley and he received a telegram to join the surveying expedition in Sinai under Newcombe supervision. They officially were conducting archaeological investigations, in order to hide the true reason that was related to military motivations.[90]

---

[87] *Ibidem*, p.18.

[88] *Ibidem*, p.89.

[89] Woolley, Lawrence, op.cit. The desert of sin was published for the first time as an annual handbook under the project Palestine Exploration Fund, which in that period was led by the Colonel Newcombe, which asked for Woolley and Lawrence when they were in the mission in Carchemish and then Hogarth talked to Newcombe of this two particular guys.

[90] S. Mousa, op.cit., p.6.

In August 1914, Woolley and Lawrence wrote to Newcombe, to ask for an occupation at war. Indeed, when the I World War broke out Lawrence, who was in England, asked for a position. In the meantime, Newcombe talked to General Edgar Cox to put the two of them in the Intelligence Services and their name on the list of reserves.

In the end, Lawrence talked to Hogarth for pushing the process and after 5 months in December, Lawrence was appointed as officer to the cartography in Egypt.[91]

From this point, Woolley and Lawrence entered the Military Intelligence Service in Cairo, where Lawrence used his memory of the places and the archaeological activity to resolve the disparate tasks assigned to him.[92]

"The Desert of Sin" was published for the first time as an annual handbook under the project Palestine Exploration Fund, which in that period was led by the Colonel Newcombe.[93]

---

[91] R. Stephan, op.cit. p.21.
[92] P. Knightely, op.cit., p.68.
[93] *Ibidem,* cit.p.68.

IT WAS WRITTEN WHAT WAS MEANT TO BE

UNDER THE ARAB BUREAU

When the I WW blew up, Lawrence was in England, so he tried to join the army. Before that Lawrence, since he was a child, had studied military doctrines: As previously said, he read, Mahan, Foch, Clausewitz etc. He tried to join the Officer training Corps, but he enlisted to fulfil reports and maps.[94]

After Hogarth to Colonel Headley introduced him, the Head of the Geographical section at War Office, Lawrence started on 23rd of October of 1914. Specifically, he was appointed as second lieutenant interpreter. He had an office at Cairo, and he was translating Arab place names to set up on the chart.[95] The Lt. Col. S.F. Newcombe talked to General Cox of Lawrence arrival. In December 1914, he was posted to Cairo, where he joined the Intelligence Department. During the next two years, his personal interest in the region was further developed through research and work on maps and intelligence reports. He quickly became the department's expert on Middle East; he was keenly interested in the prospects of an Arab revolt.[96]

The G.H.Q was at the Old Savoy Hotel at Cairo, he, as first soldier arrived, was considered as insignificant, but in the end he was in charge of being the Liaison Officer at Cairo between

---

[94] R. Aldington, op.cit., p132.
[95] *Ibidem*, cit p.156.
[96] J. Wilson, op.cit. p.6.

the Survey Egypt and Military Intelligence, especially after the Arab Bureau.

He had a particularity, that everyone around him was stimulated by the effect of his presence. The period in Cairo was defined as the glorious one. Sometimes he was interrogating spies and collecting information as well.

Gertrude bell, when she came at Cairo and saw him again, she said that Lawrence was quite far different from the last time.

From 1914 to 1918, he became a British hero; he was physically stronger than what he could seem with his low height and slight body; he was assistant to Leonard Woolley and was able to drop his feeling of racial superiority and get on terms with Arabs and some Kurds. However, behind there was a pre-calculation of relationships; in fact, some of them never became more intimate, because he knew very well how to use people. History had not been made up of truth, so useless would be worry about that.

In the book The Seven Pillars of Wisdom, he depicted how the cell was composed and the tasks.

"They were few people, and nearly all of them rallied round Clayton" in Sir Archibald Murray's intelligence section.[97] Clayton was the chief of the Intelligence, civil and military, service in Egypt. Clayton made the perfect leader for such a

---

[97] T. E. Lawrence, op.cit., p.56.

band of wild men as they were, Lawrence said. Clayton was a calm, detached, clear-sighted person, who had unconscious courage in assuming responsibility. He gave an open run to his subordinates. He had a vast knowledge; and he worked with his influence. He knew how to be a charismatic leader and to descry his influence was not easy at all. His way to be could be similar to the water that creeping silently and insistently go through everything.[98]

Another character of the cell was the oriental Secretary of the residence, the most brilliant Englishman in the Near East: his name - Ronald Storrs. He was subtly efficient, despite his diversion of energy in music, letters, sculpture and painting. Storrs sowed what reaped.

Afterwards, George Lloyd entered the group: he gave confidence; he was good at numbers and had a big knowledge of money. He proved to be a sure guide in those political and trade affairs looking at the future arteries of the Middle East.

Mark Sykes with his instincts that lay in parody and that saw the odd in everything was another important character, which ideas were beyond the normality, but, unfortunately, he lacks patience.

Another character, which was the mentor for all of them, was Hogarth. He was considered as their adviser, he brought them

---

[98] *Ibidem, p.*56.

lessons of history, moderation and courage. He was their referee; their untiring historian and he could be considered as a peacemaker as well. Behind him stood Cornwallis, a rude man, strong and temperate. However, Newcombe, Parker, Herbert and Graves were other characters in the cell.

The name they gave to the group was "Intrusive", due to the action to break into the acceptance and build a new people in the East.[99]

Lawrence was charged with the distribution of the Turkish Army and the preparations of maps. He added also the invention of the Arab Bulletin, a secret weekly record of Middle Eastern politics and of necessity, which the first number was created in February 1916.[100]

---

99 *Ibidem* p.58-59.
100 R. Stephan, p. 22.

British Government was creating the Arab Cause based on the figure of Lawrence as the national hero and, at the same time, he was creating the national "home" for the Jews, with Balfour as fatuous sponsor.[101]

On 31st of October of 1914, Kitchner cabled the following words: "*If Arab Nation helps England in this War, England will guarantee no interests in Arabia*". It is necessary to ask automatically where and what was considered as Arabia and which Arab Nation.[102]

The role of Great Britain in the development of the Revolt should be find back in the past, during the work of the Committee Busen, which in London before the enter of Turk in the Great War, wanted to have influence on the Turkey and the Arab population. In June 1915, the Council met all together under the Chairman Sir Maurice of Bunsen, who was a brilliant diplomat, who asked the high position of the Foreign Affairs Office. He brought to the creation of some agreements with French and the separation between Zionists and Arabs. The only way to win in the peninsula was relying on the aspirations of Arabs as principal instrument of victory in Middle East.[103]

---

[101] R. Aldington, op.cit. p.173.

[102] *Ibidem*, p.176.

[103] P. Knightley and C. Simpson, op.cit., p.86-91.

In May 1916, the secret Sykes-Picot agreement was settled and shared the territories into:

- Arab State B under the English Empire;
- Arab State A under the French Control;
- Arab State as C under Italians and in the Agreement, there were also Turks and Russians.

The war brought this issue into focus. What would happen to the Arab provinces of the Turkish Empire, if Turkey were defeated? For Lawrence, the ideal solution would have been self-determination. He advocated that policy consistently throughout the war, at the Peace Conference, and during his time at the Colonial Office. Of course, he was a realist. He did not believe in Arab unity - there seemed little likelihood, in the short or medium term, that the elites of Damascus or Baghdad would accept rule from Mecca or any other Arab centre. In addition, an independent Arab administration would need a greater Power to guarantee its frontiers, or it would not keep its independence for long. New states would need to call on outside expertise to assist their development.

The Arabs were less stable than Turks were. They were politically representing a mosaic, where each piece of the ISAN was considering himself independent and as a jealous entity, unable of cohesion.

The alternative to this solution would be the colonization under the European Forces, but the problem would be the promises that Lawrence made to Feisal for the Arabs. Notwithstanding, if the Europe won, the promises would be impossible to maintain, and Lawrence knew it somehow. He knew how Arabs were and that they believed in persons, not in institutions. They saw in Lawrence a free agent of the British Government, and, for this reason, they demanded from him an endorsement of its written promises. Instead of being proud of what they did together, Lawrence was always a little bitterly ashamed, for the double game he was playing.[104]

For him was evident from the beginning that if England had won the war, the promises would be dead paper. If he had been an honest adviser of Arabs, he would have said that they should have to go to their home. However, he had an immodest presumption that he could help Arab uprising, giving them the power to be stable and defeat the European army.[105]

Nevertheless, in the inland areas behind the Mediterranean littoral, no Power other than Turkey could have any rational justification for imposing a colonial administration. The French did not agree. France had long-standing imperial ambitions in the Middle East and seemed to believe that adding huge areas of desert to its Empire would be a fit reward for its wartime sacrifice in Europe. To Lawrence, replacing Turkish rule with French would make the situation worse than that was.

---

[104] T.E. Lawrence, op.cit., p.24.
[105] *Ibidem*, p.24.

He consistently opposed these French ambitions. In the end, France did impose colonial rule in inland Syria, though that triumph was short-lived.[106]

<hr>

[106] J. Wilson. op.cit., p.6.

I decided to title this paragraph such as one of the nickname Lawrence had during his life. He was called "*the king without the crown*" because somehow, he succeeded managing the tribes, the armies, the enemies and handling the situation, although he was not the true Arab king. He was an important character in the revolt and parallel in the war against Turks and Germans. People said that the enemy in this case, Germans and Turks, offered a reward for the capture of the great guerrilla leader "Lawrence" and that the reward was up to 50000 pounds.[107] Anyhow, possibly the story of the reward might be a fake. Bedouins should accept no money, because everything was paid by trading goods: for example, the bodyguards were paid not with gold, but with dresses and camels. Lawrence was wearing good and delicate clothes, which were beautiful and expensive for Arabs. He wore a gold belt in front of which was the curved golden dagger presented to him by Hussein. In a letter of 1920 and 1927,[108] Lawrence said that the dagger was made in Mecca, precisely near the third little corner of the main bazar. The creator was an old Nedjj goldsmith, whose name was Gaesin. Secondly, how come was possible to address a message to Bedouins who cannot read?

---

[107] R. Aldington, op.cit., p.259.
[108] *Ibidem,* p.261

The doubt rose because the counterpart memories like *Jemel Pasha* and *Liman Von Sanders* did not mention this event.[109]

---

109 *Ibidem, p. 260.*

THE CONCEPT OF REVOLT

Before to start talking about the Arab revolt, a fine explanation from a strategic point of view is important. Generally, in my opinion the framework to define the revolt is vital to frame reasons and manners of Arabs fights.

Indeed, the way of fighting performed by Lawrence is also recorded in the book "Revolt to revolution: the fourth dimension of Warfare Volume II. This book, written by Micheal Elliot-Batemoun, John Ellis and Bauden, is explaining the different ways of using the revolt like a medium of war, precisely such an asymmetric warfare.[110]

Indeed, the insurgency of Arabs did not follow the concepts of the doctrine war, based on the ideas of Foch's doctrine. This dictum says that in the modern ethic is vital to seek for the enemy's army, which is the centre of the power, and the final goal is to destroy it in battle.[111]

The Arabs had fine results, but the problem after the revolt is to seek in their incapacity to be persistent in the time.[112] The consideration that comes out is that the war of the Arabs should be considered as a simple and individual conflict. A general rule says that the way of fighting sometimes reflects the mentality of the population engaged in the conflict. They were

---

[110]M. Elliot-Batemoun et all, *Revolt to revolution: the fourth dimension of Warfare*, Volume II. Manchester University Press 1974, p.146-150.
[111] *Ibidem*, p. 145.
[112] *Ibidem*, p. 160.

not fighting for the IWW, but they were just fighting for the defeat of Turks.

War is and always has been a persistent form of political intercourse between tribes. There are many types of attacks, wars and conflicts, but formally, military organizations have been reluctant to recognize guerrilla as a form of warfare. Superficially, it should be considered more like a form of insurgency or internal disturb. Indeed, Mao Tse Tung pointed out that formal warfare is concerned with the direct and external attacks. However, this concept may have value 50 years ago or more back in the past. After all, taking advantages from a revolt, I can start a military action or make the head of the State weaker. The basic assumption of Guerrilla was the effective capacity of destroying from the within something.[113]

Main features of this movement were their spontaneity, lack of organization and lack of effective leadership in a political sense, which eventually were all features present in the Arab tribes. In Europe, backwords, strikes and industrial disputes became more frequent as wage-earns.[114]

An early attempt to put military affairs before the political ones without contradictions in revolutionary theory occurred by chance through T. E. Lawrence. He should not be considered as a rebel; on the contrary, he was an archaeologist, who took

---

[113] *Ibidem,* p. 4.
[114] *Ibidem,* p. 5.

part in some excavations in the Mesopotamian area, where he developed an extraordinary knowledge of Arabs life and culture. Properly for this precious treasure, he was recruited to participate in the revolt, where Lawrence understood that instead of traditional military philosophies, which were inoperative, he needed to develop a guerrilla system.

Regardless, the next step in the desire of Lawrence to give a state after the revolt was impossible, since they were conducting a simple and individual war for the freedom and the removal of Turkish presence. As far as this last sentence is concerned, there is a sentence used by Lawrence when he was sitting in the tent of Feisal that clarify the desire of Arabs to expulse the Turks from their land.

The problem was probably in the failure of creating a solid administration and in the opposition of the Great Powers to put Feisal at the lead of Syria.[115] In the end, the movement could not cope with the realities of urban government, international challenges and political interests. When Lawrence withdrew from Middle East affairs in 1922, his letters written later, displayed that he continued to believe that self-rule was better than imperial rule, and that great powers should not deprive another people of self-government - even if that self-government was far from perfect.[116]

---

[115] *Ibidem, p.* 5.
[116] J. Wilson, conclusions.

Some examples might be listed like the first that at the height of the Arab revolt in Palestine a British Intel Officer arrived and intended to form a Jewish army coincident with the Jewish characteristics: his name was Orde Wingate. He first created the special *"night squad"* consisting of British and Jewish soldiers who outfought the Turks in northern Palestine. His main efforts were directed towards the creation of a Jewish Officers' cadre with distinctive military philosophy.[117] Obviously, at the same time they were promising to Arabs a land just for them through the words of Lawrence.

The historian Aaron S. Klienman said that the responsibility come from a decision, that was the claim of territories for the creation of Tampon State, for the protection of Egypt. Indeed, Kitchener understood the lesson learned after the success of the attack of the Turks in February 1915 through the Sinai. Turk column used the canal of Suez and let the troops retire in the strip of Gaza. What frightened Kitchener was the presence of Russia and France in the Mediterranean Sea that link to the presence of India through the Suez Canal created an unstable international balance. Therefore, the principle of the strip of Gaza, and consequently the creation of Palestine, was the creation of a tampon State and the Jewish State to support the Navy with the infrastructures and harbours in Haifa, from

---

[117] M. Elliot-Batemoun et all., op.cit., p.23.

which the railway was cutting the country until high Mesopotamia.[118]

In October 1916, he has been sent on an Intelligence mission to the Hejaz. This led to a permanent attachment as British liaison officer with the irregular Arab army commanded by Sheriff Feisal. He remained with these forces until the fall of Damascus in October 1918.[119]

---

[118] P. Knightley and C. Simpson, op.cit., p.86-92.
[119] J. Wilson. op.cit., p.7.

The beginning of the Arab Movement had started in Mesopotamia, under the impulse of *Seyid Taleb* and later under *Yasin el Hashimi*. In the meantime, Lord Kitchener was approaching an Arab idol for his gestures, called *Aziz el Masri*, who was the *Enver's rival*, the Turkish enemy. A good moment for the Arab revolt was after the defeat in Ctesiphon, when the troops of Townshend needed help and they sent Lawrence to advise him against the Turks. In that moment, people living in *Nejef* and *Kerbela*, were in revolt against *Halil Pasha's* Army. The surviving *Halil Pasha's* Army were not loyal anymore to him as well.

In January 1916, Lawrence received a mission in which he could consider as the most estrange of the English military history. He was almost 28; he was working as a subaltern officer and simple agent of the Intelligence Service. He was designed as attaché to the Expeditionary Corp in Egypt, in Cairo. The mission was assigned to him, because of a problem dating back to the previous year, in which the Indian Army, aimed to protect the oil camps in *Masdjid-I Sulayman*, decided to give the protection of this infrastructures to an army composed of Indian and British men, under the overarching command of Townshend.[120]

---

[120] P. Knightley and C. Simpson, op.cit., p.75.

He landed his troops at *Fao* and he occupied *Chatt al Arab*, but then when they moved on the formation used by Townshend was not useful for the war in the desert; resulting in a difficult idea of attack and occupation of Baghdad. At *Cteiphon*, Townshend jumped into the Anatolian column of Turks, commanded by Commander *Halil Pacha*, counsellor of the *Marshal von Der Goltz*, an old German superior officer who participated in the recognition and deployment of Turk Army in the desert.

On 29th of March of 1916, General Robertson sent to Townshend, via telegram, an information saying that they are sending from the Egypt supports. He arrived at *Bassora* around the 30th of March for giving advice and finding a convenient mediator. However, the solution was founded on a political level. Lawrence was angry for the fact that there was no military solution instead.[121]

When he returned to Cairo, Lawrence submitted a report about the situation in Mesopotamia, in which the Colonel Stirling was criticizing the mission in general and as well as the ways and tools for the operation.[122]

---

[121] *Ibidem*, p.75-80.
[122] R. Stephan, op.cit., p.22.

THE MEETING WITH THE TRUE KING OF THE DESERT

In October 1916 Ronald Storrs, oriental secretary at the Residence in Cairo, came to Djedda, for examining the possibility to help in the most effective way the revolt. Lawrence in "The Seven Pillars of the Wisdom" expressed his angry for the fact that the solution was not a military aid, but using political lines.[123]

In that period the most important personality in the desert was the king Hussein, who had four sons to whom divide his Empire. Lawrence was looking for someone who can lead the revolt and take the crown of king for the Arab population and the creation of the first Arab nation. In his book, he described the moments visiting Hussein's sons to find the right personality.

At first, he found Abdullah too wise and intelligent; Ali was too sweet, Zeid was too cold; and then, there was Feisal. He found in him the possible and future chief, who had both the right skills, the right spirit and the right capacity of savoir-faire that could boost the Arab population in the uprising against Turks and merge tribes together for State building process.[124]

He found only in Feisal the right person, because when he met the other brothers Abdullah was high skilled in a political

---

[123] P. Knightley and C. Simpson, op.cit., p.97.
[124] *Ibidem*, p.98.

conduction typical of tribes. He learned by his father, and Lawrence said that he lacked franchise. Abdullah to the other part did not want that Lawrence had influence on the Bedouins tribes. While Lawrence was listening to him to analyse his person, he described him as too clever. Feisal, on the contrary, was tall, with a remarkable beauty an manners, but not with the same attitude to the politics as his father or his brother.[125]

The Colonel Clayton, who led the Arab Bureau, ordered him to come closer and closer to Feisal with the aim to understand and manipulate him. Otherwise, Lawrence did not want, he knew it could be dangerous. Thus, from London arrived the decision to place Lawrence as Political agent beside Feisal.

The book I with the title "the discovery of Feisal" goes from chapter VIII to XVI, within Lawrence remembered the first time he met the Sheriff of Mecca, Hussein, and his sons. While he was writing, he was following the entire order in which he met them.

Afterwards he rode up the country to Feisal, and Lawrence found in him the leader he needed with the necessary fire and reason to give effect to the "science" of the group created in Cairo. Here I suppose that with science the writer meant aim or goal.[126] The advantages were that Feisal had equipped man

---

[125] *Ibidem,* p.99.
[126] T. E. Lawrence, op.cit., p. 135.

and the natural geography from his side, only Jebel Subh was Feisal's flank threat.

In accordance with lines written by Lawrence, in his book the first son he met was Abdullah, and Colonel Wilson, the British representative in the New Arab State, introduced Lawrence.[127] He had the impression that the life was very merry for Abdullah. Abdullah was a short but strong man, with a carefully trimmed brown beard. He was charming on acquaintance and when they fell in serious discussion, the veil of humour disappeared, and he normally chose his words arguing shrewdly.[128]

According to the public opinion of Arabs, they thought that Abdullah was a far seeing and astute politician. His goal was to win the Arab independence and he used the rumours trying to grant the group acceptance. Anyway, his ways and his manners did not convince Lawrence and Storrs completely. Lawrence, in fact, thought that what Abdullah lacked was the enthusiasm, which later would lead to a lack of leadership. Abdullah did not have for Lawrence the flame that would set the desert on fire.[129] Lawrence found Abdullah too balanced, too cool, too humorous to be a prophet, especially the armed

---

[127] *Ibidem,* p.67.
[128] *Ibidem.*
[129] *Ibidem,* p.68.

prophet. Feisal was for Lawrence a figure too complex for a simple purpose.[130]

After the stay in Jedda, they left the city by ship to Rabegh for the meeting with the second son: Ali. The boat was an Indian marine ship, on board there was the liaison officer. Ali was of middle height, thin and looking already more than 37 years. His skin was shallow, his eyes large and brown, and his nose thin. He had excellent and admirable manners.[131]

Beside Ali stood Zeid, his young half-brother, who was helping him at Rabegh. Instead of the brother, Zeid was shy, white and beardless, calm and flippant, no zealot for revolt. Zeid was less than Abdullah the born leader of Lawrence quested. Lawrence knew that Zeid would be a decisive man when he would have found himself.

Ali maintained secret the Lawrence departure; they let him leave after one day, due to the presence of possible bands under *Hussei Mabeirig*, the ambitious Sheikh of the clan who now was a fugitive and there was the order to send Lawrence to Feisal.[132]

In addition to this, Ali gave Lawrence a white cloth and a camel. Then Lawrence, Ali and *Tafas* left to reach the Feisal Camp. Their journey was complicated for Lawrence who

---

¹³⁰ *Ibidem.*
¹³¹ *Ibidem,* p.76.
¹³² *Ibidem,* p.75.

passed from two years sitting behind a desk in an overcrowded office at Cairo, to walking down in a desert, where the sun shines so long, and the environment conditions were extreme. They passed from a district to another until *Tafas* reached his home one: *Masruh*. After that, they passed through the *Wadi Mared*, then the *Bir Ibn Hassani* and after stayed at Khallaf's place who was an old garrulous camel-rider who told them about the last fighting in which Feisal was involved.

They knew that *Khallaf* was under the Turkish pay to talk and count each person who was passing from *Bir El-Hassani*. The group travelling went also through the sands and detritus of *Bir el Sheikh*. Afterwards, the more they were reaching the Feisal territories, the more landscape around changed. Now the colour was green with cliffs of unusual colours.

Then they arrived at *Wadi Safra* and its biggest village *Wasta*. In that period, *Wasta* was a populous village of the Wadi (Valley). There were thousands of houses, but then a wall of water rolled down *Wadi Safra* and swept away many gardens and houses. For this reason, the dwellers moved to a tiny settlement a little above Wasta, called Kharma.[133]

On 18th of October of 1916 the travel to Feisal was coming to the end, in fact, after Kharma, finally they arrived to Hamra

---

[133] *Ibidem*, p.92.

where a slave let Lawrence and the others enter an inner court. There stood a white figure waiting for him.

Brighton, which was with Feisal, said nothing and Lawrence was the only vocal witness. It is surprising that a king is waiting nervously for an emissary of the English Empire. Notwithstanding, Feisal for Lawrence was fated to lead the Arabs to the defeat of the Turks and the establishment of their independence.

Probably for this reason, Lawrence was considered as the heaven-sent military genus to guide him. Lawrence after Feisal death said that he was a timid man, he hated running into the danger, but he would have done anything for the Arab freedom.[134]

In the Seven Pillars of Wisdom is written that Lawrence:

> *"felt at first glance that this was the man he had come to Arabia to seek – the leader who would bring the Arab revolt to full glory. Feisal looked very tall and pillar-like, very slender, in his long white silk robes and his brown head-cloth bound with a brilliant scarlet and gold cord."*[135]

Lawrence continued describing Feisal's nature:

---

[134] R. Aldington, op.cit., p. 195.
[135] T.E Lawrence, op.cit., p.90-95 and R. STEPHAN, op.cit.

"his movements were impetuous. He showed himself hot-tempered and sensitive, even unreasonable, and he ran off soon on tangents. Appetite and physical weakness were mated in him with the spur of courage. His personal charm, his imprudence, made him the idol of his followers".[136]

He was fuller of wit than of humour, because training in Abdul Hamid's entourage had made him good at diplomacy and the military service improved his relation facing the Turks. This training had given him a knowledge of tactics. He was a careful judge of men and fulfilled his journey and the aim of his trip.[137]

Feisal was crossing his fingers above his dagger, and when Lawrence greeted him, Feisal made way for him into the room; a tiny and dark room, where there were little figures staring at both, when they were sitting and waiting for talking.

Feisal started asking for the travel, he also asked if he liked *Wadi Safra*. Lawrence talked about the sun, the heat of the desert and at the question if he liked Wadi Safra, Lawrence answered sharply, like a sword in their midst. Indeed, he said:

"well, but it is far away Damascus".[138]

---

[136] *Ibidem*, p.98.
[137] *Ibidem*, p.98.
[138] *Ibidem*, p.92.

"praise be to God, there are turks nearer us than that" Feisal smiling said.

In the meantime, Sir Reginald Wingate was sent from Sudan to the Egyptian major Nafi Bey with his soldiers to help the Arab rebellion. The battery was there because Wilson heard about the history of Feisal and his brothers to whom was promised a mountain artillery battery.[139] Indeed, the history is connecting with the fugitive Hussein who decided to link with Turks and not to go supporting Feisal.

Therefore, the four brothers were separated; Abdullah in mecca, Ali and Zeid in Rabegh, but Feisal came to Hamra, to rest disgusted by the impotence of Arabs. Lawrence thought immediately to the comparison between Arab English and Arab German.[140] Hussein wanted to put away from the Arabian Peninsula the Turks and made Arabs rise. Firstly, he sent his three sons to determined places. Feisal was sent to Damascus, where he found three divisions ready for the rebellion, the second son Ali was sent to Medina with his brother Zeid and he found two divisions in Aleppo. The third one, Abdullah, should sound the British by letters. Anyway, anything of what planned came out, because Turks destroyed the plan before, so Jemal Pesha entered Damascus and Feisal was searched for hanging.[141]

---

[139] *Ibidem,* p.94-96
[140] *Ibidem,* p.94-96
[141] *Ibidem,* p.49.

Lawrence also asked about Feisal plans for the attacks against Turks. They were convincing, recruiting people from the tribes and even from the Turkish Army, concerning those soldiers not happy of the Giant Empire decadence.[142] Lawrence saw how the Ottoman Empire was going to die; they were still linked to traditions that were replaced with new scientific ones.[143]

They went out the court and Lawrence wanted to see Feisal's followers. Hence, before leaving, Lawrence walked down the lines of the troops and wanted to feel the flame of the soldiers. It was the moment of the farewell, where Lawrence told to Feisal that he was coming back at Cairo, he probably knew about the possibility to meet again, but he wanted to highlight that the work at Cairo was not related to field's work. He said that he would have talked to his officers and chiefs about the situation, and that probably there would be a second chance to meet again. Feisal appointed to Lawrence a guard to *Yenbo*.[144]

From Yenbo Lawrence was writing constantly reports on the Arab situation, especially to Sir Wingate, who from years was dreaming to have some affairs in this revolt, and here is the explication that from Sudan Wingate sent some agents to help with expertise the Arabs movements. Clayton liked the reports Lawrence did as well. He was considered as a good and

---

[142] *Ibidem,* p.97.
[143] *Ibidem,* p.54.
[144] *Ibidem,* p. 110 -115.

pungently observant, and since that officers and chiefs in the Arab Bureau in Cairo had been treated him better than before.[145]

Once came back from Hejaz in October at Cairo, then he was ordered to come back and stay close to Feisal. The first time he went to him in an unofficial way with Storrs, and especially he said that work at desk at Cairo has nothing linked to the work on field.

During these months, within Lawrence was searching for the new leader of Arabs, the revolt broke out on the 5 June 1916, while according to Abdullah on 10th June 1916. After the first failure, however the information and the knowledge Lawrence had about Turks forces deployment was extraordinary.[146]

On the 9th of June of 1916, the Sheriff of Mecca started the uprising against Turks. The situation that Lawrence planned it came true. He had to wait one month before entering the scene of war.[147]

On 28th of June of 1916, the English Empire backed Arabs Troop with two battery for mountain. In July Rabegh and Yenbo withdrew and then on 22nd of September Taifa as well. Lawrence was jotting down each note on the book II that regards the Arab offensive.

---

[145] *Ibidem,* p. 110-115.
[146] R. Aldington, op.cit., p.194.
[147] R. Stephan, op.cit. P.23.

The second book concerns the opening of the Arab offensive, when Clayton, after few days told Lawrence to come back to Arabia and Feisal. This time the travel was to Yenbo, the new special base Feisal's army. Here Garland, who was an enquirer in physics and had practical knowledge of explosives, was teaching rebels how to use the dynamite to blow up railways.

Then they moved to another spot, this time suddenly Lawrence started the chapter with the request of Feisal in wearing Arab cloths, which made Lawrence grateful for the request. He described different aspects of Feisal, and gradually he was reconstructing his personality. He said that Feisal was using simple and direct words, when he was speaking to his soldiers in dialects. When Lawrence wrote about him, it was possible to see more emphasis, underling movements and observations.

In chapter XXII he dwelt at the particularity of Arabs, depicting them quiet but confident, they are compared to lizards on the soil of the desert, proud and full of a sense of patriotism, but in mass they were not so formidable, for the reason, they had no corporate spirit, nor discipline nor mutual confidence.

The smaller the unit, the better its performance. A thousand of Arabs were ineffective against Turks forces. However, three or four, hidden in the hills, they could cope with 12 Turks.[148] Napoleon already noted this with the mamelukes. During the

---

[148] *Ibidem*, p.140

1916, they had to leave Yenbo and move to north, through Wadi Messarih, towards Owais. Then they rode up for other more days, passing through many valleys with wells and hills.

The actions were like in a ping-pong match, a city was conquered and another lost. After Owais they captured Whejd. Lawrence opened his third book with this victory and the Turks that abandoned the advance towards Mecca for a passive defence of Medina and its railway.[149]

Envier was advised to evacuate medina and Sir Archibald Murray begged the troops to cut the retreating enemy with a sustained attack. Unfortunately, when everyone was ready, Lawrence felt ill and he could do a little for the railway.

The second step of the plan was to reach Abu Markha, where Lawrence gave the documents from Feisal to Sheriff Abdullah and explained the railway offensive actions. It was the period, which Lawrence spent in his tent and wanted just to lay down to get rest. He thought an hour it could feel better, even if in the end, he laid down for ten days. He was affected by happy fever and dysentery.

He suffered a bodily weakness. As usual, he reported that in those circumstances his mind cleared, in fact, his senses became more acute. He began to think about the Arab Revolt, looking for an equation between book reading and movements.

---

[149] *Ibidem,* p.170.

He called out in his mind the most important theories and figures like Napoleon, Clausewitz, Moltke, Clemmer as well as he thought to possible modern and scientific way of warfare.[150] When he restored himself, he understood why he was dreaming to fulfil his mission.

He came back to Feisal, finding the Yenbo camp that changed. During this long time, he was always jotting down notes regarding many aspects of the Arab world, he met many people on his way and he resumed in one page the Bedouins manners and hospitality.

"The Arab war was geographical. The aim was to seek the enemy's weakest material link and bear only on that time. The Bedouins were unused to formal operations, but they had assets of mobility, toughness, self-assurance, knowledge of the country and an intelligent courage. The greatest economy they had was life, the life was more important than money or time. If they were patient and superhuman skilled, they could follow reach the victory. They must not take medina, because the Turks were harmless there".[151]

In autumn 1916, objectives for the British Empire were well defined as first Medina and then Akaba. This city might be a vital harbour in the red sea for the use of submarines and the launch of mines. In addition to this Akaba was an important

---

[150] *Ibidem*, p.193.
[151] *Ibidem*, p.231-232

base for Arabs against the invasion of Syria. On 14th of December of 1916 General Wingate, George Llyod and Bremond met in Khartoum and decided that Akaba and Wejh must be occupied because considered as bases against the railway and obstacle the work of Turks and Germans.

The plan was conducting asymmetric attacks, that means raids and surprise attacks to blow up bridges and railways.

On the 4th of December of 1916, Lawrence met again Feisal. This time Lawrence was wearing white Arab clothes. The first raid started on 12th of February of 1917, out of Wejh. When Major Garland and his assistant blew up a train and a bridge. On the 3rd and 4th of March of 1917, another successful attack was conducted and led by Colonel Newcombe. Lawrence made his first raid under the guidance of Captain Raho, who taught him how to use the dynamite on 28th of March of 1917. He was frenetic when he touched for the first time the iron of the railway that blew up. The plan was simple and consisting in going to Akaba and once there to cut the railway. The Arabs needed Aqaba; firstly, to extend their front, which was their tactical principle; and secondly, to link up with the British Army.[152]

According to the Arabs, Aqaba spelt plenty in food, money, guns and advisers. For Lawrence the revolt had to reach the main battle against Turkey, if not it would be considered as a

---

[152] *Ibidem,* p.281.

failure and he told to Feisal that freedom should have taken, not given.

The first raid started an hour before noon. Nasir was the leader, riding his Ghazala, a camel well vaulted and huge ribbed as an antique ship; towering a good foot above the next of our animals, and yet perfectly proportioned, with a stride like an ostrich's - a lyrical beast, noblest and best bred of the *howeitat* camels, a female of nine remembered dams.[153]

Unfortunately, for months, Aqaba was considered the horizon of their minds, and then when they entered the village, they discovered that Aqaba was all a ruin. Repeated bombardments by French and English warships had ravaged the place into simply a war-torn village. Apart from the country folk, the six great towns vital in that period were: Jerusalem, Beirut, Damascus, Homs, Hama, and Aleppo.[154]

Fortunately, Lawrence had the master key for each of the city visited and for the heart of all the people, which he met in Syria and around the desert: it was the Arabic language, his experience and his way of communicating. There were distinctions, but those were political and religious. Since their childhood, they were lawless, only they were obeying to her father for physical terror. Arab population did not believe in Institutions, but in people.[155] However, the most important

---

[153] *Ibidem,* p.288.
[154] *Ibidem.*
[155] *Ibidem,* p.341-342.

element, the Patriotism, was warped to the language, as to the soil of race.[156]

After the attack and the capture of Aqaba, the rebels pointed to the second step that was the railway just above Zerga. The Circassia village north of Amman.

The hot sun and fast riding had tired their camels and Zaal decided to water them at a ruined Roman village where the underground cisterns had been filled by the late rains. There was a military post of two tents on a tall bridge just down the line as well. The Turks seemed active and the cause, as later heard, that a general's inspection was pending. The goal was to destroy the bridge that was near the Turk camp.[157]

After rebels captured Aqaba, the Hejaz war ended, and gave them the opportunity of helping the British invading Syria. The Arabs working in Aqaba became virtually the right wing of the Allenby's army in Sinai.[158]

On the 4th of October of 1917, Lawrence wrote more about his thoughts, days spent thinking about the organization and strategy with Feisal and new operations went forward in his mind. It was the moment for another strike. Otherwise, in that occasion Lawrence made a reflexion about the fraudulence of his business, especially becoming the principal actor of the

---

[156] *Ibidem,* p.344.
[157] *Ibidem,* p.293.
[158] *Ibidem,* p.320, Book V.

revolt. He was raising the Arabs on false pretences and exercising a false authority over his duties. He conducted the mine pose after a bite of a scorpion. He made the comparison of this problem with the interior crime he was committing to be a false leader. The internal pain was roving him by inside, as the venom of the scorpion does.[159]

He said that upon this text:

> *"his mind went waving across its dusty space, amid the sunbeam thoughts and the dancing motes of idea to endure by orders or because it was a duty. He considered himself as a theft of souls to make others die in sincerity for his graven images; it is heroic to have offered up his own life for a cause in which the person does not believe it. Arabs because they accepted our message as truth, they were ready to be killed for it; a condition which made their acts more proper than glorious, a logical bastard fortitude, suitable to a profit and loss balance of conduct. To invent a message and then with open eye to perish for its self-made image – that was greater".*[160]

When I have taken for the first time the book, titled "The Seven Pillars", dated in 1961, I had noticed that there were just few parts underlined and that beside the paragraph was written

---

[159] *Ibidem*, p.387.
[160] *Ibidem*, p.567.

something concerning the Bible. It was surprising how some concepts and some sentences were perfectly matching with passages of the Bible or the books of Matthew, Luke. An example that may fit the concept he expressed was at page 395 in a verse of the Bible Matthew, (6, 24):

> *"Not for the first- or last-time, service to two masters irked me. The concept that it is possible to serve just one with full devotion".*[161]

The most beautiful one is the explanation of why the title is "the seven pillars". If it could be reality, it would be interesting understanding why Lawrence wrote following the Bible.

Lawrence talked about himself and thought about his thirtieth birthday, what he dreamed to be and meant to be. He was craving for good reputation among men, but his situation was fretting him inside. He was suspecting of himself because everyone trusted him, Arabs, Clayton, and Allenby. He was playing a triple game. This let him start thinking that everything was set on fraud. He was not modest, but ashamed of his awkwardness and of his solitary unlikeness, which made him no companion, but an acquaintance, angular and uncomfortable.[162]

---

[161] *Ibidem*, p.395 and verse of the bible. There is in the popular movie of Lawrence of Arabia this sentence quoted as well. When Feisal and Lawrence are standing in the tent and Feisal asked who Lawrence was serving and affirmed that it is impossible to serve two masters.
[162] *Ibidem*, p.579.

There was the craving for being popular, but he decided to be independent as others and inside himself, all the time opposite feelings were present. Feelings and illusion were at war within him. He was a man whose delight lays in the desire and when a thing was in his reach, he no longer wanted it. He had special attraction in beginnings, which drove him into everlasting endeavours to free the personality from accretions and fresh medium, that his curiosity to see its naked shadow might be fed.

However, there were qualities like courage that needed a medium, and even if everything was based on an egoistic curiosity, this way meant to be to express the Lawrence's qualities.[163]

Day by day, everyone was learning and practising the art of mining. In the last four months, experts from Aqaba destroyed seventeen locomotives. Travelling became an uncertain terror for the enemy and at Damascus people scrambled for the back seats in trains, even paid extra for them. The terroristic actions led to civilian traffic nearly ceased.[164]

At the same time, Allenby was recreating the broken British army, asking what both railway efforts and Wadi Musa meant, because Turkish messages showed an interest in attacking that part. Lawrence answered that they should made a trap for

---

[163] *Ibidem,* p.583.
[164] *Ibidem,* p.389.

Turkish army. For him no spies cannot count them because they were treated as a regular and formal enemy, when they in practise had different ideas of movement and tactics. Instead of the Arabs, who know each of the Turkish single unit and every man they move. Bridges and railways were blowing up continuously and the goal to cut each way of communication was producing his effects.

In the regular Arab forces, there was no power of punishment whatever: the vital difference showed itself in all troops, which had no formality; there was no subordination. Service was active; attacks always imminent, and like the army of Italy, men recognized the duty of defeating the enemy. For the rest they were not soldiers, but pilgrims, which intent was always to go the little farther.[165]

In January 1918, Lawrence was in the middle of his battle in which his knowledge of tactics and the study of Clausewitz and Foch helped him to win the battle in the last line of defence of Tafileh.[166]

After the action in Hesa and Amman that let they enter the city wearing women dress, they scouted the city, the planning of Maan attack was the following step. The description of Arab

---

[165] *Ibidem,* p.522.
[166] *Ibidem,* p.490-492.

ways of thinking that is possible to understand nowadays was already written in Lawrence's masterpiece.[167]

The final step of the revolt was concluding with the strike for the conquest of Damascus. They finally would have won, even if the city were completely ruined. The step forward was to create a cohesion and for this reason some institutions and service for the citizens. The goal for Lawrence was leaving and sailing from Syria with a clear sky and everything fixed with Feisal king of Arabia.[168] After the war, Damascus was normal: there were shops, street merchants trading, a prison and even a security force consisting of one brigade.

When Damascus fell, the eastern war ended. Even if many fronts still existed, the war was a tussle in a turnip-field. The eastern war was considered in Seven Pillars as the main one the contribution to the war in Middle East came from Lawrence and the Arabs, led by political and personal motives. The political one was that Anglo - French coalition shared the territories and established the homelands for Arabs and Jews.

The latest moment of Lawrence in Arabia is dated on the 8th of October of 1918, when Lawrence returned to Cairo, after he came back Europe to fight on the western front.[169]

---

[167] *Ibidem, p.567.*
[168] *Ibidem, p.620-683.*
[169] *Ibidem, p.291.*

Once Lawrence came back Europe, the person who made of him a legend was Lowell Thomas.

Indeed, he made of Lawrence of Arabia that symbol on which Arabs put their hopes for freedom. The freedom in the dreams of both Lawrence and Arabs was depicted like the end of the rivalry among tribes for the land in a free and united nation.

The truth appeared in the reports Lawrence wrote that at the beginning of the revolt was to take under control the Arabs uprisings and guarantee the order. There was a report written by a sub-lieutenant attaché to the Intelligence Service, which described clearly the way of conduction of the revolt. This was a confidential report for the General Staff at Cairo, called *"The politics of the Mecca. PRO, FO, 414/461"*.[170]

---

[170] *Ibidem*, p.291.

PERIOD AFTER WAR

After the end of the war and the revolt, the most important war was conducted in the rooms of the Hotel Majestic and the Orsay on 18th of January of 1919 during the Conference for the Peace.

Lawrence, tried to do in the mission the best he could to maintain the trust of Feisal, and at the same moment, manipulate the movement to the best interest of England. Once he left, Lawrence found a substitute to put beside Feisal. Indeed, an Arab become the player of the Lawrence's double game. He was *Aouni Abdoul Hadi*, getting a place in the delegation of Feisal and assigned to the Foreign Affairs Ministry. It is said that the new right wing of Feisal had a change with Lawrence of some private letters. Political lines wanted that Lawrence was to bring Feisal on the right way for the interests of the European powers.

On 20th of March of 1919 during the Peace Conference, the destiny of Syria was discussed, and in the conference, George Llyod and the Frenches participated with other interests. Indeed, behind the Sykes-Picots agreement made Syria a French Government puppet State.[171]

Feisal was told he should go to Paris to discuss the agreements. There were General Gouraud and Feisal on the other side. Feisal did not accept the ultimatum until the 14th of July of

---

171 R. Aldington, op.cit., p.297.

1920, day of the repression of the Arabs. Damascus was occupied and Feisal fled away leaving the instauration of a military dictator.

Feisal wanted with all strengths to protect and preserve the State of Syria, but everything changed in some months when the French troops entered and expelled the King Feisal from the Capital (Damascus). The dream of a Syrian nation unified and free disappeared.[172]

---

172 P. Knightley and C. Simpson, op.cit., p.201.

Once back to the ordinary life, he came back to Oxford. The only situation within he wore a uniform in England was when he entered the R.A.F and the Tanks Corps.[173]

In 1919, the Secretary of State for War was Sir Winston Churchill, whose attention to Lawrence was attracted by someone who said he was a wonderful young man. Hence, Sir Churchill invited Lawrence to dinner. Unfortunately, the attraction for this young figure turned into disapproval because he gave back the King George V medal, since he said that Arabs were sacrificed to the demand of French for Syria. However, the more probable version of facts is that he refused for the promise he made to Feisal.[174]

Another event important was his flight crashed near Rome: the two pilots died, and on the contrary, he survived, but he was severely injured. Indeed, he broke some ribs and hurt his collarbone. He also lost his second draft of the Seven Pillars of Wisdom and started writing again from the beginning.[175]

Before the meeting, Churchill and the popularity of Lawrence grew up thanks to the figure of Kingmaker war Mr Lowell Thomas.[176] Gertrude Bell, the queen of the desert, was more known than Lawrence was. Nonetheless, within few months of

---

[173] R. Aldington, op.cit., p.292.
[174] *Ibidem*, p.310-311.
[175] *Ibidem*, p310-311.
[176] *Ibidem*, p 20.

August 1919 Lawrence was known as the King of Arabia or the Prince of Mecca.

When Mr Thomas got to Jerusalem, which was conquered in 1918, he found a shaved man, with a dagger and wearing beautiful white Arab clothes. Therefore, inevitably, his curiosity was drawn by that figure and he came directly to Storrs, asking who that blue-eyed fellow walking down the street among bazaars was.[177] Storrs, before he could finish the sentence, disclosed the door and said the uncrowned King of Arabia, the Bedouin Prince, absorbed in a toe of Archaeology.[178]

Lowell Thomas, who met Lawrence in the holy land in 1917, started a series of conferences in England on the topic of the revolt in Arabia and his success. Lowell Thomas presented to the Western Culture the Arab Revolt as an adventure without shadows. For Lawrence the Arab Revolt was a political movement within the essence was a fraud, as he wrote in the letter n° 214 of 15th of August of 1923.

In another letter n° 103 of 15th of July of 1918, he wrote about himself as a thief of opportunity and that everything was a godless fraud.[179]

---

[177] *Ibidem,* p 324.
[178] *Ibidem.*
[179] R. Stephan, op.cit., p.72.

Afterwards, Lawrence in April 1919 was victim of an aircraft accident where part of the notes for his book were lost for the second time. Indeed, he started writing a second version of his masterpiece "The Seven Pillars of Wisdom", in 1919, which he finished the second version in September 1920. The first version had been started to write in June 1914. Amid the 1921 and February 1922, he redacted the third version of his masterpiece, and in July 1922, the Oxfordian Institution published eight templates of "The Seven Pillars of Wisdom".[180] Gertrude Bell played also an important role in the life of Lawrence boosting him in the publication of his work. She suggested that other copies of the masterpiece should have been printed.

Beside this start as a writer, in the end the relationship between Churchill and Lawrence changed again when the Prime Minister decided to invite and use the knowledge of Lawrence as the only local expert in Arabia. In May 1920 a rebellion in Iraq blew up and they spent one month to instil in the mind that the king should be Feisal, if they would have avoid having bombed their territories.[181]

In February 1921, he was appointed as counsellor of the Secretary for Colonies for the Arabs Affairs and he attended the conference in Cairo and in Palestine. After 5 months, he

---

[180] *Ibidem,* p.30.
[181] R. Aldington, op.cit., p.348.

was appointed as plenipotentiaries for the agreements with Hussein, the king of Hedjaz.[182]

---

[182] R. Stephan, op.cit., p.29.

Once back in England, he felt he was missing something, and this was the adventure; the piece of life he left in the desert. For this reason, on 30th of August of 1922, Lawrence joined up at Henrietta Street the R.A.F. with the name John Hume Ross, his matriculation was A/C 2, n°352087.

In the meantime, on 27th of December of 1922 he became famous as the king without crown, even if he was just a simple soldier. The title was published on the Daily Express. [183]

Afterwards, Trenchard asked him to be an officer, but he refused. On the contrary, he asked the permanent dismissal. After this, he joined up the Royal Tank Corps under the name of T.E- Shaw, and his number of matriculations was n°7875698.[184]

In 1927, he was in Karachi, but then he returned after two years. Mr Thurt asked for the identity of Lawrence, by that time on the Daily News an article title the great mystery of the Colonel Lawrence was published with the label definition of the Arche-spy.[185]

On 26th of February of 1935, he was finally demobilized; retiring, he left for Clouds hill. Indeed, in October 1923, he

---

[183] *Ibidem,* p.31.
[184] *Ibidem,* p.32.
[185] *Ibidem,* p.34.

bought a house on Clouds hill, which was a chalet ruined not far away from the military headquarter.

The book is opening with the preface of A.W Lawrence, in which he explains that the title seven pillars is not something aleatory, but it might be associated to what is written in the Bible, in the book of Proverbs (IX. I). Indeed, the proverbs says that the:

> *"Wisdom hath builded a house: she hath hewn out her seven pillars".*[186]

The younger brother also says that the title the Seven Pillars can refer to the seven cities he visited. For the first text says he wrote books number 2, 3, 4, 5, 6, 7 and 10 when he was in Paris, around the period that comes from February and June of 1919. The introduction after he received some reports by his chiefs in Cairo, in July or August and then when he was in England, he wrote book 1. He used his war notes, which he destroyed after he had used them.

Just three people read them before he lost everything. There were some similar events, at first, he lost his notes at Reading station, while changing trains during the Christmas period in 1919 and then during the air crash near Rome.

The text I was around 250,000 words, instead of the Text II, which Lawrence started writing again and was around 400,000

---

[186] T. E. Lawrence, op.cit., p.15.

words. He corrected the time lapse with the information of the Arab Bulletin and other two diaries that survived.

The third text, instead of the previous ones was composed with great care, it was nearly 330,000 words long and it was begun in London, written later in Jeddah, then in Ammam during 1921 and again in London in February 1922. There are two versions of that: the privately printed texts and the published ones.[187]

The first category was about 8 copies printed textually, in sheets, at Oxford, in the first quarter of 1922, by care of the Oxford Times staff. Eight copies were required and five copies more for the Hejaz Expeditionary Force that was created in order to read it critically for him and that should have been destroyed later. In the end that it had not been done. About the copies, he only knows how many copies he had given. Newspaper statements said 107, but it was possible that were more than 107.

In the introduction, Lawrence stated the essence of the masterpiece:

He is not here to deliver lessons addressed to the world or to shock people. The history is of myself in the Arab movement and in the daily life with little things and little people.[188]

---

[187] *Ibidem,* p.16.
[188] *Ibidem,* p.22.

He was afraid that they paid too much for something ruined by other people. Lawrence opinion was that they paid too much in honour and innocent lives.

He was supposed to lead a young mass of Arabs in support of English, without having a true vision. Then the Arab experience opened Lawrence's eyes. Eventually he was thinking of being near those men able to see through two veils at once, two environments or two educations.[189]

According to Lawrence, Bernard Shaw improved every paragraph. Lawrence had considerable gifts as both rhetorical and propagandist writer. Unfortunately, he lacked spontaneity, naturalness and tact of omission. He was persuasive and plausible advocated with decided taste and ability.[190]

The Seven Pillars was such a success story, but told as Lawrence tells it, in his rhetorical style and ramification; it had to be diluted and suitable.

The Style of Seven Pillars is not Pseudo-Elizabethan. On the other hand, Doughty's influence may be to blame for the confused structure, with long-winded digressions, the ruthless translation into the chosen idiom of every detail jotted down as notes.

Camel is a better word than *thelul*. On the other hand, Lawrence liked Doughty writings. Sometimes he forgot – that

---

[189] *Ibidem,* p.30.
[190] R. Aldington, op.cit., p.359.

his reader may not share his interest in endless descriptions of obscure desert features and persons. He created suggestions: an example was the word "clean" to appeal to puritan prejudices when he spoke about Farraj and Daud, who were a homosexual couple in the desert. Lawrence praised the sword as symbol of war.[191]

His way of writing and the rhythm were fast as well as the war. War is action, so speeches should be vigorous, direct and unaffected.[192]

There was one achievement which nobody can deny to Lawrence, and that was his capacity to convince others that he was a remarkable man. Of course, he was, but what was chiefly remarkable was his capacity for self-advertisement. He was a soldier among writers and a writer among soldiers.

Lawrence was a determined and ambitious, succeeding in impress such eminent persons such as Sir Winston Churchill, Madame Forster, and Mr Lewis Namier. The tragedy of Lawrence's life was the inner conflict started by the shock of discovering the secret, which was never resolved. He was thinking on the Christian egoist who thinks that universe was designated for damnation or salvation.[193]

---

[191] *Ibidem,* p.377.
[192] *Ibidem,* p.378.
[193] *Ibidem,* p.399.

The literature was not a simple pretext to ludic activities, but it was a way of vowels and consonants to go out and matching. In Lawrence, the English text was characteristic for the power of self-expression in some imaginative form. The literature was considered like the psychoanalysis, the meaning shown could reveal a blurred and latent meaning. The true narrator writes like a Christian that confess his sins, like a patient talking to the doctor.[194]

He did for first time allusion to his book in a letter to Doughty in November 1919, when he started the second version, because he said he lost his manuscript of his adventures in Arabia. It was stolen from him in the train. Therefore, he should start writing again, letter n° 117 of 25th of November of 1919.[195]

When he finished the book, he expressed two different judges in two letters, n° 167 on 7th of September 1922 *"the worst is I am dead tired, and the disappointment of the seven pillars, if you knew how rounded a pearl of my conception of it has thinned my temper"*. In the second to E-M Forster n° 243 on 20th of February of 1924 where he was writing that his thing was forced from him not as a poem, but as a complete narrative of what happened in the Arab revolt.

---

[194] R. Stephan, op.cit., p.64-65.
[195] *Ibidem*, p.69.

To sum up, He ended to depict a psychological description of Arabs in his masterpieces.[196]

In March 1927, there was the publication of another work: *The Revolt dans le desert*, which was sold around 40,000 copies. In 1928, he started the translation of the Odyssey and in 1928, he stored his notes on R.A.F., these were published in 1955 under the title "The Mint" (*La matrice*).[197]

---

[196] Ibidem, p.103.
[197] *Ibidem*, p. 34.

Beside the masterpiece and other pieces of work, he wrote, there are some letters, that before were considered restricted or private, and then that were published.

Below there is a list of the letters and some parts of the contents.

- To V.W. Richards: he was that person with who Lawrence decide to buy a press machine. The first letter was on 15th of July of 1918. It is a ridiculous letter, but that it could be an aspiration for next changes, and that he needs rest like purgation and then meditation to take the right way to be. He compared himself like a bobbin of a film where there are black and white colour created by the elements he found around.[198]

- Teo Robert Graves: on 04th of February of 1935 where he explained his work in the army, why he was not satisfied, then why he entered again in the R.A.F where he could not understand all the mechanism as well as his relationships with women.[199]

- To Ernest Thurtle: on 26th of April of 1929, he was born in 1884 and he was a labourism deputy, who was fond of ancient battles and published a book about the military

---

[198] R. Stephan p.170-172.
[199] *Ibidem,* p.174.

discipline and democracy. Lawrence wrote to him about his last moments when he retired at the age of 35. [200]

-       To Lionel Curtis: on 19th of March of 1923. Lionel Curtis was born in 1872 and he was working at the Colonial Office. Thanks to him, there were outrages about the Commonwealth, the war and the China.[201]

-       The first one sent on 19th of March of 1923 at Bovington Camp was the preparation to the series of letters called the mill letters. The first one ended with an exclamation in French in which he exclaimed, *"Quelle vie!"* Meaning that was the life of men which were in a civil war and the way to find the harmony was long.

-       The second one was sent on 27th of March of 1923, which was in a moment of reflexion, where he stopped himself looking at barracks

-       The third one was written by the Tank Ville base on the 14th of May of 1923. Lawrence wrote about his free time, in which he tried to meditate, to leave his spirit run freely and passing from thought completely different. He repeated that when his mood was down, he jumped on his motorbike and started driving fast with the wind in his hair.

This was possible to appreciate in people who came back from great adventures, great situations, great landscapes and they

---

[200] *Ibidem*, p.175.
[201] *Ibidem*, p.175-190.

could not find the normality and accept it, until they would not reach any strong feeling. They try to enjoy and test that they are alive, which is the only precious thing in the world.

> *"He said that he wanted to risk that thing that is Worthing 2 shilling and 9 pence for day."*[202]

-        The fourth one was written on 30th of May of 1923 and the fifth one was written on 27th of June of 1923.[203]

[202] *Ibidem, p.175-190.*
[203] *Ibidem, p.170.*

He had an incident on 13th of May of 1935. On that day he was coming back home riding his motorbike, when he had an accident with two people riding their bikes. He hit with violence his head and he has been in coma for 5 days. Then he died on the sixth day, even because if he could wake up, he would have lost his memory, nor he would have been paralyzed.[204]

Many people had different theories: natural death or complicities causes, because of his new book full of Secrets of State, or killed by Germans, Arabs and French. Alternatively, that everything was false, just to send him under different name around the Arab world and accomplish his missions.[205] Lawrence was the appropriate hero for his class and epoch.[206]

Lawrence has been captured by the adventure and by his companies: he was English when he had his first victory against Turks, he was happy when he became Arab. After Sykes-Picot Agreement, he lived with a sense of dissimulation, wearing a mask. Nevertheless, he wanted to be remembered as Arabs saw him: trusty and loyal.[207]

He was buried on 21st of May of 1935 under the Church of Moreton. Eric Kennington made a bust for him, which was

---

[204] *Ibidem*, p.37.
[205] P. Knightley and C. Simpson, op.cit., p.398.
[206] R. Aldington, op.cit., p.441.
[207] R. Stephan, op.cit., p.53.

placed in the dungeons under the Saint-Paul Cathedral. His chalet in Clouds hill passed under the National treasure for visitors.[208]

The desert was a place for the epiphany, a place where to stay alone and think, finding loneliness and revelation. Eventually, not only vanity existed.

---

[208] *Ibidem*, p.38.

CLOSING NOTE

To sum up, Lawrence may be many figures, an archaeologist, a spy, a student, a rebel, a lieutenant, a writer, a poet, a king of the desert, but for sure, he was a person who became a legend and that all around the world know even at distance of a century. This dissertation has retraced Lawrence's lifetime and his literary works, recollecting all the information in an easy version for everyone. The reconstruction of the history has been difficult, because sometimes everything seems to be wrapped in a blurred magic mist, where understanding if it was reality or just pure imagination is complicated, or even as it happens in the desert like a mirage.

It is possible to say that the desert is a place of revelation and only strong people can cope with this hazardous environment. Lawrence was one of them, he may be considered a dangerous person, as it is said in the movie "Lawrence of Arabia" everything was written in his mind and not only vanity existed.

Therefore, what really mind is who people are and what they do, how they are living, if they are kind and with a huge servant heart. These are all the ingredients to become a legend and do something extraordinary.

Eventually, one day the coincidence will meet the fate:
"Look who I ran into" the coincidence crowed
"Please", in the end the fate flirts "this was meant to be".

Antonino cambria

Do mojej kochani, ktòra jest moim skarbiem.

BIBLIOGRAPHY

- Aldington, R., *Lawrence of Arabia,* Penguin Books, 1971.

- Doughty, C. M., *Travels in Arabia Desert, with an introduction by T. E. Lawrence*, Volume I, Dover Publication, Canada, 1979.

- Elliot-Batemoun, M. et all, *Revolt to revolution: the fourth dimension of Warfare, Volume II*, Manchester University Press 1974.

- Knightley, P. and Simpson C. and Laffont R., *Les Vie Secretes De Lawrence D'arabia*, 1970.

- Lawrence, A.W., *T. E. Lawrence by His Friends, Biography*, War Collection, 01.01.1937.

- Lawrence, T. E., *Crusades Castles*, preface by Franco Cardini, Introduction by Denys Pringle, Cahiers, Castelvecchi, 2018, Translation by Maria Grazia, Chiappori, Roma.

- Lawrence, T. E., *The Seven Pillars of Wisdom, a Triumph*, Penguins, 1962.

- Moorey, P. R. S., *Cemeteries of the First Millennium B.C. At Deve Huyuk 1980, Near Carchemish (Jerablus)*, Salvaged by T. E. Lawrence and C.L. Woolley, 1913.

- Mousa, S., *T.E. Lawrence an Arab view*, translated by Albert Butros, London, Oxford University press 1966.

- Stephan, R, *Thomas Edward Lawrence, par Roger Stephan*, collection "La Bibliotheque Ideale", Gallimard, 25.04.1960.
- Wilson, J., and National Portrait Gallery, *T. E. Lawrence, Lawrence of Arabia*, 1989.
- Wilson, J., *from a dream to a legend*, paper, 2011.
- Woolley, C. L. et Lawrence, T. E., *Le Desert de Sin*, introduction of Sir Frederic Kenyon, Payot, Paris 1927.

WEBGRAPHY
- Rigsby, Dr Rick, Pep talk, how to make an impact, 2019. https://www.youtube.com/watch?v=UGyKmiySTv8;
- Wilson, J., *From a dream to a legend*, paper, 2011. http://www.telstudies.org/discussion/youth_1888-1914/wilson_tel_from_dream_to_legend.shtml;